# BETWEEN COURAGE AND COWARDICE

## Choosing to Do Hard Things for Your Own Good

Rev. J. Ronald Knott

*Sophronismos Press*
*Louisville, Kentucky*

# Between Courage and Cowardice
*Choosing to Do Hard Things for Your Own Good*

For information address:
Sophronismos Press
1271 Parkway Gardens Court #106
Louisville, Kentucky 40217

Cover Design & Book Layout:
Tim Schoenbachler

First Printing: September 2018

ISBN: 978-0-9962445-6-5

# Also by J. Ronald Knott

*All books published by Sophronismos Press*

## BOOKS FOR CLERGY

**INTENTIONAL PRESBYTERATES:**
*Claiming Our Common Sense of Purpose as Diocesan Priests*
(Spanish and Swahili editions available)

**FROM SEMINARIAN TO DIOCESAN PRIEST:**
*Managing a Successful Transition*
(Spanish edition available)

**THE SPIRITUAL LEADERSHIP OF A PARISH PRIEST:**
*On Being Good and Good At It*
(Spanish & Vietnamese editions available)

**INTENTIONAL PRESBYTERATES:** *The Workbook*

**A BISHOP AND HIS PRIESTS TOGETHER:**
*Resources for Building More Intentional Presbyterates*

**THE CHARACTER OF A PASTOR IN EXERCISING AUTHORITY**

**PERSONAL GROWTH PLAN:** *A HANDBOOK FOR PRIESTS*

## HOMILIES / SPIRITUALITY

**AN ENCOURAGING WORD:** *Renewed Hearts, Renewed Church*

**ONE HEART AT A TIME:**
*Renewing the Church in the New Millennium*

**SUNDAY NIGHTS:** *Encouraging Words for Young Adults*

**AFFIRMING GOODNESS**

**THE LORD IS CLOSE TO THE BROKENHEARTED**

**A PASSION FOR PERSONAL AND VOCATIONAL EXCELLENCE**

**OUR JOURNEY OF LENT**

## FOR THE RECORD BOOK SERIES

**FOR THE RECORD:**
*Encouraging Words for Ordinary Catholics, Volumes I - XV*

*For information about eBook and printed editions of Father Knott's books, go to:* www.ronknottbooks.com

# DEDICATION

To my friend, Patrick Murphy –
I was talking to him when "I woke up!"

# ACKNOWLEDGMENTS

I would like to thank Mr. Tim Schoenbachler who assisted me by giving structure to my writings, editing the text, designing the cover and layout of the book. Without his help this endeavor would not have been possible.

# Table of Contents

# *Preface*

*What is most personal is most universal.*
Carl R. Rogers
American Psychologist

This book is filled with personal stories – very personal stories. I knew going into this project that there is a risk in sharing so much of myself with so many people. In sharing my stories in this way, I know that I am risking rejection, being seen as different and out of step with the majority of the world, or my particular experiences being perceived as so strange and foreign that people cannot relate to any of the things I have experienced.

Because I am a Catholic priest and have lived all of my life as part of a spiritual culture, it might seem that my personal journey and experiences would not be very similar to the average person. However, because I am a human being I share all the complex emotions, hopes, dreams, doubts and desires that are part of the human condition.

I have learned from almost fifty years of preaching and writing that, in the words of Carl Rogers, "What is most personal is most universal." In taking this risk of sharing so many intimate and personal stories, I believe that what I have learned from my experiences may indeed be of help to others.

I also know, in the words of the famous baseball player Johnny Sain, that "People don't want to hear about the labor pains, they just want to see the baby." People are not interested in what I have been through unless my handling of those experiences can be presented to them as helpful in some practical and obvious way. I hope that my insights are helpful to those who face difficult decisions in their own lives when they are at a critical point that might alter their path for better or worse. *How* one handles things that need to be handled is often more important than *what* needs to be handled.

If I thought my experiences were merely unique to me, I would not have written this book. If I thought my experiences were unique, this whole effort would simply be an embarrassing exercise in narcissism. However, I sincerely believe that while the particular events mentioned here may indeed be exclusive to me, the opportunities that were given to me and the decisions that I made in response to those situations, whether they be from courage or cowardice, could very well be more universal than I suspect they are.

In this book I will talk a lot about courage and cowardice. The best description of the battle between courage and cowardice that I have found comes from Marrianne Williamson.

"Our deepest fear is not that we are inadequate. Our deepest fear is that we are powerful beyond measure. It is our light, not our darkness that most frightens us. We ask ourselves, 'Who am I to be brilliant, gorgeous, talented, fabulous?' Actually, who are you not to be? You are a child of God. Your playing small does not serve the world. There is nothing enlightened about shrinking so that other people won't feel insecure around you. We are all meant to shine, as children do. We were born to make manifest the glory of God that is within us. It's not just in some of us; it's in everyone. And as we let our own light shine, we unconsciously give other people permission to do the same. As we are liberated from our own fear, our presence automatically liberates others."

I have always understood courage and cowardice as polar opposite responses to fear. For me, courage is knowing what needs to be done and choosing to do it no matter what, while cowardice is knowing what needs to be done and choosing not to do it no matter what.

This whole book is filled with stories of breakthroughs on the other side of what appeared to be breakdowns. There is a famous joke about a child who wakes up on Christmas morning and is surprised to find a heap of horse manure under the tree instead of a collection of presents. Yet, the child is not discouraged because he has an extraordinarily optimistic outlook on life. His parents discover him enthusiastically shoveling the manure as he exclaims, "With all this manure, there must be a pony somewhere!" The point is that things are not always as bad as they seem. My hope in sharing my stories is that my readers, in reflecting on the unfolding of their own lives, may have had the same experience as the unknown author of this quote, "Sometimes, when things are falling part, they may actually be falling into place."

Another reason for writing this book, besides the possibility that someone may be inspired to stand up to their own fear and cowardice, is that it gave me a chance to do a "whole life review." In the words of Flannery O'Connor, "I write because I don't know what I think until I read what I say." By sharing what I have learned, I solidify what I know. It is not lost on me that I am only five years away from my 80th birthday so it might be good to do it now while I can still remember it. Even now, there were certain "important" events that I could not seem to put a date on without a little research.

In this book, I use many quotes I have collected in the personal journals I have kept over the years documenting my efforts at intentional personal growth. I find them to be extremely useful pearls of wisdom. They come from some of the world's most insightful writers and thinkers.

By way of introduction, here is a sample of those guiding insights as they pertain to courage and cowardice.

"Being terrified but going ahead and doing what must be done – that's courage. The one who feels no fear is a fool, and the one who lets fear rule him is a coward." – Piers Anthony

"Courage is being scared to death but saddling up anyway." – John Wayne

"The cave you fear to enter holds the treasure you seek." – Joseph Campbell

Public speaking may be the most obvious area where I regularly face my fear and choose courage over cowardice. I have lost count of the number of dioceses to which I have traveled to lead seminars and retreats for priests. I know it is well over a hundred dioceses in ten countries. Every time I get on a plane to do yet another one of those engagements, I am surprised at myself and wonder how I got to this point in my life. In my gut, I know it is not brains, but a deliberate choice of courage over cowardice. I have learned this important lesson: choosing to do hard things for my own good has enriched my life in astounding ways.

Abraham Maslow, a renowned American psychologist, was so right when he wrote, "We crave and fear becoming truly ourselves." On one hand we want to become all that we can be, but on the other we want to avoid the work and possible criticism that serious change entails. In the face of the fear of becoming truly ourselves, Ralph Waldo Emerson offers an important warning. "God will not have his work made manifest by cowards." In face of our craving to become truly ourselves, he also encourages us to bravery. "Do not go where the path may lead, go instead where there is no path and leave a trail."

# BETWEEN COURAGE AND COWARDICE

## THE MOMENT OF GRACE

*All human nature vigorously resists grace because grace changes us and the change is painful.*

Flannery O'Connor

Sometimes, in a matter of seconds, the course of our lives may change dramatically because a sudden insight becomes so crystal clear that we know we are at a crossroads and we know how we choose to respond to it will alter our life's trajectory. Such an insight came to me in the spring of 1966. I was extremely bashful. I avoided meeting new people or getting myself into unfamiliar situations. I was scared of life. I was what George Bernard Shaw called a "feverish little clod of grievances and ailments, complaining that the world would not dedicate itself to making me happy."

A fellow seminarian, Pat Murphy, and I were standing on the fire escape outside the third floor hallway window getting some fresh air between classes. We were sharing our feelings about some of the expectations of the "seminary culture" in which we were living. The seminary staff was expecting me to "develop my talents." I was, no doubt, sharing something about my inability to "fit in."

In what had to be one great moment of grace, an impulse gift from God, I suddenly blurted out, "Pat, I am so sick and tired of being bashful and scared of life that I'm going to do something about it even if it kills me!"

I was shocked by the words that came out of my own mouth. But from that moment on, I have been standing up to the coward in me. I have been deliberately "slaying dragons" and "confronting demons," in my head and on my path, ever since. I would not be where I am today if that particular great "moment of grace" had not happened and if I had not responded enthusiastically. I decided that day not to indulge my resistance to personal and spiritual growth anymore. That day, on that fire escape, I made my first conscious decision to enter the world of personal growth and deliberate living. How appropriate and symbolic that the decision was made on a "fire escape."

That day, on that fire escape, I finally learned a fundamental principle of personal and spiritual growth – fear and pain cannot be used as excuses for backing-off from life. I have come to understand that pain serves a purpose. Pain captures our attention and lets us know that change is necessary. Pain signals that it is time to move on and learn new behaviors. Unfortunately, many of us sabotage the possibility of growth by denying, numbing or backing away from such pain.

Ask any person with a rich and full life to look back over the events of their life, and chances are there will be a turning point of some kind. All the other events of their life, either before or after that pivotal moment, will refer back to that event. For me, the fire escape experience was that pivotal moment.

Some may call these turning points or pivotal moments, "luck" or "an opportunity coming from nowhere," but as a believer, I would call them "moments of grace." Grace, as Webster defines it, is "unmerited divine assistance given to human beings for their regeneration." Even so, those "moments of grace" have two parts. One part has nothing to do with us personally. It is a spontaneous gift from God that shows up when it shows up. We cannot create it, capture it or force it to happen. The second part has everything to do with us personally. It has to do with our cooperation, our ability to seize the moment and step up to the plate in doing our part to see where it takes us if we follow its invitation.

We all have "moments of grace" – moments when unmerited divine assistance is offered to us for our growth as human persons. In sharing my "moments of grace," let it be known that they are unique to me. My hope is that my sharing of these with others, will trigger an awareness of their own "moments of grace" and how they have, or have not, cooperated with them in enriching their own lives.

My fire escape moment was most significant for me for this reason. I was raised to believe that "life is something that happens to you and all you can do is make the most of it." I was taught to be grateful for what I had even when it was not the best life God had to offer me. Thomas Merton was right on target when he said, "The biggest human temptation is to settle for too little." I have always wondered how my life might have unfolded if I had responded differently to that moment of grace. I realize now that I was not entirely aware of the full implications of what I was choosing in that moment.

# A PERSONAL HISTORY

## HINDSIGHT

Most of the stories shared in this book are stories remembered in hindsight. Most of us understand things better from hindsight. We don't appreciate water and electricity until it is cut off for a few hours. We always seem to have more good things to say about people when they are dead than when they are alive. Kids don't seem to realize how wise their parents are until they grow up and leave home and have children of their own.

In the same way, Scripture is hindsight. Based on an oral tradition of stories passed from generation to generation, the written texts came years after the actual events. Our ancient ancestors in the faith used to ask as they went from slavery to exodus to exile, "Is the Lord with us or not?" They were not always sure if he was with them because they experienced so much turmoil and misery. It was only after years of reflection that they were able to look back and say, "The Lord was indeed with us!" In hindsight they could see how God was acting in their journey.

As I celebrated forty-eight years of priestly ministry on May 16 of this year (2018), I know that I understand what priesthood is about more today than I ever did fifty years ago. What has helped me more than anything is hindsight. I may have felt God's absence on any given day or given month but looking back from here, I can see clearly that God has indeed been present and active in my life as a priest.

From hindsight, I will share personal stories showing how I responded unconsciously to many moments of grace in my life before that fire escape experience and how I have responded consciously with an intense deliberateness and enthusiasm to subsequent moments of grace ever since. I am sure there were many times when I did not, or could not, recognize the moments of grace offered me, but I was trying to seize the moment when I sensed one was being presented to me.

# THE UNCONSCIOUS YEARS

*Surely the Lord is in this place,*
*and I wasn't even aware of it!"*
Genesis 28:16

## The Omen

My earliest memory of wanting to be a priest goes back to 1950, the year Fr. Henry Vessels was ordained a priest from my home parish. I was barely six years old. I don't remember attending his first Mass, but I do remember one particular day soon after his ordination. He was visiting one of his sister, the wife of a farmer who used to cut my hair. I was there at the house that day for a haircut.

Father Vessels had taken off his Roman collar and laid it across the bed in the front bedroom. He was in the kitchen playing cards at the table with some of his relatives. I was waiting for my haircut in the living room between the kitchen and the bedroom. Bored as I waited to get my haircut, I sneaked into the bedroom, picked up his collar off the bed, held it up around my neck and tiptoed to look at myself in the mirror. I remember doing it quickly because I thought that I was committing a sin, just by touching that Roman collar!

That episode happened almost seventy years ago, but I can still remember the smallest details, even to the point of being able to reconstruct how the furniture in the room was arranged. It took twenty more years to actually get to my ordination. After seventy years, I can look back and say with confidence, "Surely, the Lord was in that place, and I wasn't even aware of it."

# The Poster Validation

As a child, I was very bashful, a bashfulness that would last through my seminary college years. I liked to be invisible. Being dragged into the light of people's scrutiny was terrifying.

In the second grade, in 1951, Sister Mary Ancilla instructed us to draw a poster for a possible entry into the regional Fire Prevention Poster Contest. I remember so many things about it very clearly. I drew a two-part poster with two children playing with the fire in a fireplace on the left half and one of the children in a hospital bed on the right half. There was a mother standing beside the bed with a big spoon and a medicine bottle in her hand with huge tears coming out of her eyes.

Not too long after I turned my poster in to Sister, she called our house and suggested to my mother that I come to the convent on Saturday to "touch up" my poster because she thought it ought to be entered into the regional contest. I remember being hesitant. I was honored to be invited into the big parlor of the convent on a weekend – something that was very, very, very rare in those days. Even disciplinary problems were dealt with during school hours. I "touched up" my poster as instructed with a bit of dread. I remember thinking, even at that age, that by becoming that visible regionally, I was setting myself and Sister up for disappointment. I was very conflicted by the whole incident, but I gave in and sent my poster to the judges.

To my surprise, I was the winner of the regional fire prevention poster contest. I remember both dreading and looking forward to the award ceremony. The whole school was assembled in the cafeteria for the presentation of my award – a valuable, in those days, "Parker Pen and Pencil Set."

## The Vocation Declaration

In 1952 I remember "going public" with my hunch that I wanted to be a priest. I remember clearly the moment when Sister Mary Ancilla asked us second-graders what we wanted to be when we grew up. I even remember my thought process. I was about to say "priest," but I hesitated. I knew that I could be made fun of for such a "kiss up" answer to the nun who trained the altar boys, but I remember deciding to say it anyway – even if I had to face ridicule. "I want to be a priest!" No one had encouraged me to think about being a priest. It sort of came from "within" me as if it were second nature. Looking back, I see that moment as an act of bravery in the face of all my fears.

It did not end there. After my courageous public announcement, I proceeded to flunk the altar boy test – not once, not twice, but three times! I remember Sister Mary Ancilla's exact words. I even reminded her of them at my First Mass 19 years later! "Ronnie, you are a good kid, but I don't think you will ever be any good around the altar!" It was more a statement of frustration than a prophetic statement. I never held it against her, but I did make her sit in the front pew at my First Mass!

## Gone Camping

In 1956 I was in the sixth grade. I was an active member of the Conservation Club at school. It was really a club for kids who loved to hunt and fish, swim and hike. None of that really appealed to me, except maybe playing in the woods and swimming. I had only shot a gun once in my life and I used to fish a little in farm ponds. I think what appealed to me mostly was the opportunity to go on a trip to summer camp at Camp Currie on Kentucky Lake. I was ready to "get out of Dodge" even though it meant being with people I did not know, doing things I had never done before and being away from my family for the first time for a whole week. I might have been the first boy from my home town willing to sign up for a summer camp, much less actually go. It was very scary, but for some reason I was drawn to do it.

## Top Chef

Throughout grade school, I was known to "play church" and conduct "funerals" for dead animals. My older sister and I were constantly creating "circus acts" and putting on "plays" and "talent shows" in the back yard. I was comfortable "leading services" and being "on stage." Of course, that was easy in front of an audience of one sibling in a town of twenty-seven people, but it was the stirring of some deep-down feelings that would surface in spades in the years to come.

In the seventh grade, I was an active member of the 4-H Club at school. We were all encouraged to develop a new talent and then give a "demonstration" of that talent at a county-wide competition at Meade County High School in Brandenburg, our county seat. Boys normally gave a "demonstration" on things like shearing a sheep, building an above ground storage facility for silage or building a chute to load cattle or pigs. Girls normally gave a "demonstration" on knitting or quilting, canning or building a "cold frame" for germinating plants for the garden.

I decided to give a "demonstration" in baking bread! I was actually baking a bit in those days: cakes, pies and cookies. I remember thinking, even then, if the "priest thing" did not work out I would go to culinary school and become a chef. This was a very bold move for a 12 year-old country boy from Meade County. I remember hesitating several times, even hiding it from my Dad, as I prepared my loaves of bread to take to the competition. I remember very clearly deciding to face possible county-wide ridicule and be the first boy in the history of Meade County to enter a 4-H Club baking contest. It was one daring and bold move in those days especially for this bashful kid. As it turned out, my bread did not rise as much as it should, but I went ahead with the "demonstration" and focused on the mistake I made by incorporating it as part of my presentation, rather than back out of the contest or try to hide the problem. I ended up getting a purple ribbon – the highest color awarded in the contest. My bread might have been a little "dense," but the ribbon, I was convinced, was awarded to me more for bravery than baking. At the awards ceremony, I became a folk hero of sorts for my daring to break a 4-H stereotype.

## Emerald City

Sometime during the spring of 1957, just as my cousin, Bob Ray, was about to graduate from grade school and leave for Saint Romuald High School in Hardinsburg, I distinctly remember a conversation we had on the playground. In fact, I can remember the very spot on which we had that conversation. He told me he was thinking about entering Saint Thomas Seminary in Louisville that took young men right out of the eighth grade. I remember the excitement and possibilities the news of that seminary's existence stirred in my soul. I knew, right then and there, that I was going to try to "get in" as soon as I graduated from grade school, just a year away. The idea both excited and scared me.

## A Star in the East

Sometime during the spring of 1958, about the time I was scheduled to graduate from Saint Theresa Grade School, I knew that it was time to "make my move." I did not even think about following my cousin and go to Saint Romuald High School. It was "that seminary somewhere in Louisville" that I had never seen before that was the focus of my radar.

Somehow, I persuaded my Dad to take me to see our pastor, Father Felix J. Johnson, to discuss my intention of going to the seminary. Father Johnson was a hard man. Going to talk to him about anything was scary, so I decided to recruit my Dad to go with me because they seemed to get along doing business together. I don't even think my Dad made a special trip for my purposes, but he allowed me to go along because they had other business to tend to and I "could ask him while we were there." What was so amazing about the whole episode was that no one was trying to recruit me for the seminary. I don't even remember hearing a "vocation talk" from any priest or nun. My parents and none of my relatives certainly ever tried to talk me into thinking about seminary. None of the other boys of the parish near my age had ever left for the seminary.

Father Johnson's response to the news that I wanted to talk to him about going to the seminary did not go over well. He looked my thirteen-year-old self over standing there before him and said, "No! You are too young and too little. Go home and grow up first." I was thirteen years old about to turn fourteen.

Panicked, I pulled out the only tool in my toolbox. I started to cry. It must have moved him. I remember every word of what he said next. "OK, I will fill out the papers, but you'll be home before Christmas!" I realized even then that this was not the kind of reception one would expect from one's pastor, even a salty old one at that. A pat on the back and some sage advice on how to handle what was ahead of me would have been nice, but I was willing to take whatever "win" I could get that day.

Sometime during that summer, I learned that I was accepted by Saint Thomas Seminary. When I announced my good news at the Harold Vessels Country Store and Rhodelia Post Office, the man behind the cash register bet me $5.00 in front of everybody standing around that I would not make it through my first year. That was brutal, but just one of many remarks that could have tempted me to doubt my decision. There were those who did encourage me. Sister Agnes Bernard, my eighth-grade teacher, gave me the most encouragement of all. It was a bit tenuous, but it was at least a little encouragement. She told me, "Ronnie, you are going to have a hard time, but I think you can make it."

I spent the summer getting a physical, getting copies of necessary documents and gathering together the necessary things on the list the seminary had sent to my home: all clothes had to be dark colors (black, navy blue, dark gray, dark brown, dark green) no bright colors (red, yellow, orange). I still have a picture of me in my navy blue suit and bow tie standing in front of our house as we were loading my stuff into the car to go to Louisville to enter the boarding school seminary. I was going to a place that I had never seen and I would meet hundreds of boys and teachers, all strangers to me. I had my suitcase of new clothes, but I was leaving home with very little encouragement except what I could give myself.

## Rocky Road

I limped through my first year of high school seminary in 1958-1959. I was a duck out of water. I was an alien in an alien land. It took every bit of my energy and focus just to deal with the culture shock of being a little country boy in a boarding school in the big city. As a result, I was under-performing academically according to my ability. There was no such thing as counseling or tutoring. It was a sink or swim situation. They had more boys than they could handle, so "weeding" some of them out was no problem. I went home for two weeks that first Christmas and three months during the summer.

Not too long into my second year of high school, Father Joseph White, the Rector of the seminary, called me into his office. I still remember his exact words to me. "Knott. We are sending you home tomorrow. You are a hopeless case!" I stood there and cried. After all, I did not have any power. All I could do was to appeal to his mercy and sympathy. Incredibly, he gave me another chance. I sometimes wonder where I would be today if I had not cried and simply accepted his verdict.

## The Beginning of the End

During the summer of 1961, I had an experience that could be called my first inclination to start imagining myself seizing my own power and choosing to stop being a victim of my father's spontaneous outbursts. My youngest brother was born in June of that year. I was home for the summer. Late one night, he was crying from the cholic. My father was in one of his typical and often terrifying rages. I was scared he might hurt my brother who was crying endlessly. My father was yelling for him to shut up. I remember picking him up, taking him out into the driveway and walking up and down until he went to sleep in my arms. It was more an effort to protect him from harm than comforting him. I remember looking up at the stars and praying for a way to escape the madness I experienced that summer. It was like the Scarlett O'Hara, *Gone With the Wind* moment, when she returns home to her beloved planation, Tara, after the burning of Atlanta. Walking amid the ruins, she says, "As God is my witness, they're not going to lick me. I'm going to live through this and when it's over, I'll never be hungry again. No, nor any of my folks. If I have to lie, steal, cheat or kill. As God is my witness, I'll never be hungry again." I promised myself that night that I would find a way out of the madness of my life at home with my father if it killed me. From that day on, I looked for an escape route. It would take me a few more years to find it, but I believe it was one of those crucial moments when I faced my fears because I yearned for something more.

## Out of the Frying Pan

When I graduated from Saint Thomas in the Spring of 1964, the last words spoken to me came from Father White, the one who called me a "hopeless case" in my sophomore year. In Greek class, when I was having a problem pronouncing a Greek word, he said, "Knott, you have been a ball and chain around my leg for six years." I don't know who was happier, him or me, when I finally saw his face in my rearview mirror.

In the fall of that year, I entered pre-theology at Saint Meinrad Seminary for my third year of college. I was elated when I found out I was going to Saint Meinrad rather than another Sulpician seminary in Baltimore. Saint Thomas was run by Sulpicians. My experience of their formation philosophy, not necessarily the experience of others, was what I called the "dental approach." They were always looking for "cavities" to drill, focusing on my shortcomings, sins and failures.

I can still remember the orientation sessions for the new students at Saint Meinrad Seminary. They were saying things like, "We know you have gifts and talents. We are going to help you recognize them and then help you grow them." This was a new language, words I had not heard before. I found it both attractive and scary. I basically went into hiding because I was convinced that if they started digging around in my life they might find out that I did not have any. Little by little, they worked their magic on me, slowly, but steadily, bringing me to a new level of "self-actualization." I craved this kind of healthy affirmation, but I feared what it might ask of me.

## Moving Out

The Saint Meinrad magic must have taken root faster than I had realized. At the end of the summer of 1965, I had one of my numerous altercations with my father on the front porch of our house as I was about to leave to go back to seminary. I remember yelling at him, "I am sick of your craziness. This is the very last summer I am coming home!" I no longer feared my father or the ramifications of removing myself from his bad behavior. I would be free from him physically, but emotional healing from all those years of being put down would come years later. One of the first steps when one is in an abusive relationship is to "get out of the road and quit letting the car run over you," as I would counsel people later as a priest.

# THE CONSCIOUS YEARS:
## Beyond the Fire Escape

### Moving In

In the first chapter of this book I described that seminal event on the fire escape at Saint Meinrad Seminary in 1966 that has led to so many opportunities for growth and change. It was on that day, in particular, that I consciously decided to reverse my thinking - away from being a "victim of circumstances" toward being a "force of nature." With God's help, I made a conscious decision to grab life by the horns and accept God's help in making myself happy. In a great moment of conversion, I decided to do some serious changing on a personal level. What would my life might be today if God had not helped me change the way I looked at myself and the things going on in the world around me. I quit waiting for the world to change, my father to change, the bishop to change, the Church to change and situations to change. I decided to change myself from the inside out. It is a path I am still walking to this day. I believe it was at that moment that I experienced "both craving and fearing becoming my true self" most intensely.

That pivotal moment of grace on the fire escape became an affirmation of that previous summer's decision to "never go home again to live." It moved from a threat to a reality in 1966. It marked a move from making hard decisions almost unconsciously to making deliberate and conscious hard decisions for my own good. Up to this time, I was "walking by faith and not by sight." Most of the time, I was not making conscious decisions. It was purely the grace of God that was directing me. I was being led by the hand.

When school was out for the summer, I went to my sister's house in Louisville rather than go home. She agreed to let me come live in her basement while I looked for a job. I was not there long when my father showed up in his truck and demanded that I get into it and go home with him for the summer. When I resisted, he laughed and pointed out that I did not have a job or any money. My response was direct and to the point. "I would rather live in the streets and eat garbage than get into that truck with you!" He stormed out and left me shaking and trembling with the realization that I had just burned the bridge to my past without any definite plans for the future. I felt a strange mixture of dread and excitement and freedom. I didn't realize at the time what a turning point in my life 1966 was going to be.

With a place to live for a while, I began looking for work. I was able to find a minimum wage job loading trucks for Paramount Foods, a pickle-packing company near my sister's house. However, it was not close enough and transportation was a major problem. It was obvious that I needed to find a better job or even more jobs and find a place to rent within walking distance.

In a month or two, I found a job, rather several jobs, at Saint Joseph Infirmary on Eastern Parkway. I was an altar boy in the chapel in the mornings and worked on the grounds crew during the week. On the weekends, I was an orderly in the emergency room, filled in at the information desk and in medical records. I had to make enough to feed myself, pay rent on an apartment and save enough for the next school year. I was hungry a lot that summer.

With my sister's help, we found an apartment a few blocks from the hospital. A German lady by the name of Mrs. Wilhelmine King rented me an apartment in her basement for $90.00 a month. I remember sitting in the apartment after coming home from work almost overcome with happiness. No more stress. No more demeaning name calling. No more dealing with the chaos of my father's moods. I was happy for the first time in my life. I had to keep pinching myself to believe where I had arrived. As it turned out, Wilhelmine King and her husband, Paul, practically adopted me. I never paid rent again. I was able to stay at their house anytime I came to Louisville, have a meal and celebrate the holidays including their birthdays, their anniversaries and my ordination until I owned my first house on the same street in 1983 – 17 years later. I remained very close to them for the rest of their lives. Wilhelmine died in 1999 and Paul died in 2017.

## Up North

The next summer, I was between first and second Theology. In first Theology, our class picked up several new classmates who had gone to college at other seminaries or universities. It was during that fall that I met, and became friends with, Tony Taschetta, from the Diocese of Joliet right outside of Chicago. He had been doing some painting during the summers to make money. Before the school year was out, he invited me to come to Wheaton, Illinois, where he lived with his parents and help him paint during that summer. His parents invited me to stay at their house, asking only that I pay a few dollars each week for food. Tony told me we could make three or four times what I had been making doing several jobs at St. Joseph Infirmary in Louisville. Even though I had grown comfortable in

Louisville living with the King's, I decided to accept the offer and make the move.

## Westward, Ho!

Tony and I had a wonderful summer making more money painting houses than I thought imaginable for a summer job. We got every job we bid on. But at some point during the next school year in 1968, I heard of a summer program offered by the United Church of Christ called *A Christian Ministry in the National Parks* for student ministers. We would have a job in the park during the week and lead campground services in the park on the weekends. Oddly enough, I heard about it through my friend Pat Murphy who was part of my "fire escape" awakening in 1966. Pat and I signed up and attended a mandatory orientation program in Chicago. He was assigned to Yellowstone National Park in Wyoming and I was assigned to Crater Lake National Park in Oregon.

I was interested in the program mainly because I wanted some preaching experience which would not be available to me at Saint Meinrad Seminary until my last semester. On the fire escape I had committed myself to overcoming my bashfulness and this, I thought, was a golden opportunity. I could do public speaking, work with non-seminary students and have a job where I could meet a variety of people from all over the world.

We heard of a company in Chicago where we could deliver a car out west and have a free ride out to our jobs. We delivered a Lincoln convertible to Seattle. That was my first major road trip. From there, we parted ways and went by bus to our particular jobs - Pat to Wyoming and me to Oregon.

That summer, I helped open the Lodge. I drove a garbage truck at first, but my main job for the summer was night desk clerk. I also filled in as a bar tender at times, wine steward in the dining room and limousine driver to the airport and bus station. I attended several dances that were held between the Park Rangers and the student workers. I was chosen to be the Master of Ceremonies at the Miss Crater Lake Beauty Pageant!

During all this, I was going through the campgrounds on Saturday nights inviting people to come to my ecumenical campground services on Sunday mornings. I did two services each Sunday after serving at an early morning Catholic Mass. I had two other student ministers working under me: a Presbyterian music minister who led service music and an Episcopal education minister who led Bible study after the services. I always led the services and preached.

This experience turned out to be perfect for my needs – opportunities for public speaking, a fresh start in an environment where no one knew me and knew nothing about my background, a place to meet new people my age who were not seminarians, a rich ecumenical exposure and an opportunity to experience another part of the country. I didn't make much money, but I left there richer in experiences than I expected were possible going into it.

## Deaconate

I was ordained a Transitional Deacon in the spring of 1969 in the Cathedral of Indianapolis of all places. It was due to the health of the Archbishop of Indianapolis who could not make the trip to Saint Meinrad Seminary as was customary. I remember a terrible tornado hitting the city as we lay on the floor and the Litany of the Saints was sung over us. It sounded like a train. I tried not to read anything sinister into such an event. During that summer, I did my clinical pastoral education program at Saints Mary and Elizabeth Hospital. in Louisville. Every seminarian had to go through a summer "hospital chaplaincy" program to familiarize themselves with the ins and outs of ministry to the sick and dying. That summer was uneventful and not very memorable.

# THE FULLY CONSCIOUS YEARS

## The First Assignment

I was ordained to the priesthood by Archbishop Thomas McDonough on May 16, 1970 at the Cathedral of the Assumption in Louisville, Kentucky. On that day I had no clue of the role that place would play in my life thirteen years later because of the decisions I would make to deliberately choose to do even harder things for my own good in the months that followed ordination.

Several weeks after my ordination, I got a call from Father Hartman at the Priest Personnel Board saying that Archbishop McDonough was sending me to the "home missions" in Somerset in southeastern Kentucky near the Tennessee border. It was a twelve-county area the size of Delaware with very few Catholics - very few. This was very bad news. Father Thomas Buren, the pastor there, had a reputation for chewing up and spitting out associate pastors one after another. I also remember a warning from my seminary days: "Don't screw up or they will send you to Somerset." The home mission had a reputation for being a place where they sent malcontent and problematic priests. One of the things seminaries did to you back then was to 'urbanize" you. As a result, very few priests wanted to be away from the conveniences of the city even if they were born and raised in the country. Somebody had to go, and even though it was not official policy, many people thought that problematic priests were sent where they could do the least harm.

I was so demoralized when I heard the news that I called them back and begged them not to send me "down there." I remember practically screaming over the phone, "If I wanted to work in the home missions, I would have joined the Glenmary Home Missioners! It has taken me twelve years to get out of the country and I do not want to go back. I want to be able to go to restaurants, plays and movies. I want to be an associate at a place like Saint James on Bardstown Road or maybe Saint James in Elizabethtown. Please!"

Back then, there was no room for negotiation. You were expected to "obey." Father Hartman tried to assuage my irritated nerves by saying something like, "We want to create a "team" approach to the mission area and we believe you have a reputation for creativity, so we have chosen you to be part of that team." The Personnel Board heard about my summer experience in Crater Lake National Park in my final official evaluation from the seminary. It was referred to as "one of his typical creative responses" during my seminary years. Even though it was a positive stroke for my ego, I was not convinced. I dismissed it as an obvious ploy to get a sucker to go to the boondocks. A few days later, I packed my car and bought a map so I could find my way to Somerset, Kentucky, the home of Saint Mildred Church – mother church of the 12 county mission area. I was hostile and angry and disappointed.

Halfway to Somerset, I had a crucial insight, as important as the fire escape experience of 1966. I remember saying to myself, "Since I did not get what I wanted, I am going to have to want what I got. I am going to be down here for ten years, whether I like it or not, so I am going to make it the best damned assignment possible." I realized that I needed to change how I mentally approached the assignment. I needed to freely accept this difficult thing and be open to what it might teach me. If I had spent my time there in resentment and anger it surely would not have led to the opportunities that came about.

For the next five years I lived in Somerset and took my turn driving around Lake Cumberland every Sunday doing Mass out of a suitcase in Monticello, Albany and Jamestown. When not going to those small mission churches, I carried out my role as associate pastor at Saint Mildred Church. It was a relief when I found out early on that Father Buren would be moved to Louisville and Father Jerry Timmel would be his replacement to lead a new "home missions team."

During those first five years I got to do things I never could have foreseen. Besides my duties at the parish, I was encouraged to establish a campus ministry program at Somerset Community College, a University of Kentucky Extension. Because I got to know several young Protestant ministers, I was able to create an interfaith approach to campus ministry by starting a campus ministry program which pulled in several of those ministers to help. My ministry in Crater Lake National Park, no doubt, had led me to this ecumenical approach.

We created a "coffee shop" in the old Saint Mildred School. We sponsored a "hunger walk." We created a multi-sound and light show around *Jesus Christ Superstar* with the students. We had outdoor concerts. I even ended up auditing some courses and even teaching a Sociology class called "Modern Social Problems." I was a regular "show and tell" in the senior English Literature class at Burnside High School when they studied the *Canterbury Tales*. There were no Catholics in that school and they wanted to know about monks, priests and nuns mentioned in that classic piece of literature. When they got to graduation, the seniors could pick the local minister to give the Baccalaureate sermon. Even though there were no Catholics in the school, I was picked three years in a row. It might have continued if not for the fact that the local school board intervened.

I was on a roll "choosing to do hard things for my own good," but maybe the biggest "hard thing" I did during those years was to decide to go backpacking in Europe starting at Taize in France where 3500 young people per week assembled around an ecumenical monastery near Lyons. The monastery at Taize was an "ecumenical monastery" started after World War II with a mission of reconciliation among the religions of Europe. The monastery has mostly Protestant monks, but also some Catholic and Orthodox monks. Young people started being attracted to it and, little by little, the numbers swelled to the point that the monks had to try to organize it in some way. They came up with week-long retreats.

On my first trip, I took two or three students with me. We arrived in Paris on Bastille Day with no map, no hotel reservations and no guide. We had our backpacks, sleeping bags and personal tents and a few dollars in our pockets. After a week in Taize, we toured most of western Europe on the cheap, sleeping in the rain and eating out of grocery stores until it was time to fly home. All in all, I took 5 trips with 10 being the highest number of students at one time. This experience opened me up to making friends with people from around the world.

It was during my trips to Taize that I started the practice of "journaling" to document my own intentional growth. Even though it is not a daily practice, I have about 18 volumes at this time. It has been one of the most valuable practices I have adopted to follow my own human and spiritual progress. During those years, choosing to do hard things for my own good was becoming a way of life. I was doing things I never thought possible for me. I was moving from cowardice to courage as my chosen response to opportunities that presented themselves.

## Monticello

I think it was during my fourth trip to Taize in 1975 that it occurred to me that I should request a move from the parish in Somerset to the even smaller mission parish in Monticello instead of merely serving it occasionally on Sunday. I realized that I had grown too comfortable in Somerset and the time had come to "do another hard thing for my own good." I could hardly believe that I was asking to go deeper into the "home missions" that I had originally resisted so vehemently. Soon after that I was given the opportunity to be the first Catholic priest in history to live in Wayne County and to serve a newly established mission in the neighboring McCreary County.

When I moved into the basement of Saint Peter Mission Church in Wayne County, there were only 7 parishioners and the parish had $70.00 in the bank. Good Shepherd Chapel in McCreary County, another small mission church, had less parishioners and probably less money in their bank. Shortly after, I was joined in Monticello by three Sisters of Notre Dame from Connecticut and four Sisters of Saint Joseph from Connecticut who came to Whitley City. They were all "home health nurses" or "social workers" mostly – ministering to the home-bound poor or teaching in one way or another in the remote parts of the county.

During the five years I spent in Monticello the rewards of deliberately taking on that undesired assignment for my own betterment were both life-changing and energizing. What happened in those years led to some amazing experiences in the years ahead. That investment in my own deliberate personal growth is still paying dividends. Opportunities to go beyond my comfort zone were happening one after another. During those years, I was offered the opportunity to have my own Sunday radio program called "Morning Has Broken," be a volunteer chaplain in a state home for juvenile delinquent boys, start a program for youth volunteers from Louisville and Joliet (Illinois) and open a used clothing store.

In May of 1976, my mother died of breast cancer. I was very close to her. In fact, we had dreamed over the years that when my father died, she would come live with me and be my house keeper. I had visions of "spoiling her" and trying to make up for some of the years that she had been neglected and verbally abused by my father. I never occurred to me that she would go first. This unwanted turn of events, while absolutely contrary to what I expected and wanted, turned out to be another one of those "moments of grace." It opened the way to an eventual opportunity for reconciliation with my father in 1987 that may never have been there if I had had my way.

It was obvious to me when I chose to move into St. Peter Mission Church that I was not prepared to be a pastor, start a parish or raise money. One of my first jobs was to raise money for my own salary! I most certainly knew nothing about evangelization in the Bible Belt culture. In my seminary training, "evangelization" was something Protestants did. At that time priests my age were trained to be associate pastors under a seasoned pastor in large suburban parishes.

I asked the diocese if I could go back to school to learn what I needed to learn to do the job I was given. I was told that there was no money available for "continuing education." I was committed to finding a way to learn what I needed to learn on my own.

I was still going back to Somerset each week to meet with my unofficial, informal "young ministers support-group" which met every Monday in the office of the pastor of the First Presbyterian Church. There was one Presbyterian, one Catholic, one Episcopalian, one Lutheran, one Disciple of Christ and one Baptist minister in the group. We had been attending the meetings of the official Ministerial Association, which was made up mostly of fundamentalists, but found it too rigid, and though we all continued to attend, we decided we needed a parallel group of more "like-minded" ministers to meet informally.

At some point, the Presbyterian minister told us about the possibility of a Doctor of Ministry degree from McCormick (Presbyterian) Seminary in Chicago that was being offered in our area. They would send the professors to us. We would have week-long classes each semester for three years alternating between Lexington and Cincinnati, plus a major project paper and a "defense." It was proposed that we all do it together. Even though I knew it was the closest thing to what I needed to learn about Bible Belt ministry, I was reluctant on two grounds. I did not have the money and it was going to be a huge commitment of time and energy. What "sweetened the pot" was the fact that you had to connect what you were doing in ministry with what you were learning in the program and the fact that

McCormick Seminary offered me a full scholarship on two grounds: poverty income and minority religion!

Even though I was the last to "sign up," I was the only one to graduate. My thesis was entitled "How One Roman Catholic Church Dealt Assertively with its Environments." The "environments" were: external pressure and internal weakness. (1) As Catholics, we were constantly being attacked and diminished by some in the community. (2) The Catholic parishioners knew very little about their own Catholic faith. My ministry there had two fronts: external and internal. I had to try to minimize a local anti-Catholic bias that could be traced back to England. (The local Protestant population could trace their ancestry back to England from the debtor prisons through a period of indentured service on the plantations of Virginia and though the Appalachia mountains. The local Catholic population could trace their ancestry back to the anti-Catholic persecutions of England and through the American colonies, especially Maryland.) I also had to try to maximize how the few local Catholics, isolated over time, understood their own faith.

During my 5 years in Monticello we saw growth in the parish – from 6 to 96. This might not seem like much of a growth, but the priest who served this community only during the summer months had told me "not to expect any results for fifty years." We also saw a huge leap in respect for Catholics in the community at large mainly because of our social service outreach in the county. I was asked to leave my first ministerial association meeting "because I was a Catholic." When I left, the local paper had a glowing front page story about my years of service to the community.

Getting the Doctor of Ministry degree in Parish Revitalization helped me focus on building the parish and connecting with the greater community in a more intentional way. Having that degree led to my being named pastor of the Cathedral of the Assumption and becoming co-founder of the ecumenical organization, the Cathedral Heritage Foundation, a few years later.

It was during my years at Saint Peter Mission Church in Monticello that I had a significant Saint Paul type flash-of-light experience. It happened in a dream, a very vivid, memorable and life-changing dream. In the dream I was on top of a small mountain. It had no trees or bushes or rocks. It had only very short green grass like a golf green. I was sitting in a folding lawn chair and God was sitting in one next to me. We were sitting side-by-side facing the setting sun without speaking. We were both smoking cheap King Edward cigars! I knew it was God, but I was afraid to look over. We just puffed on our cigars and watched the sun set on the horizon. Finally, God leaned over and whispered in my ear, "Ron, isn't this wonderful!" I woke from the dream at that moment and the world looked forever different to me. All of the chains of fear and doubt that were holding me back had melted away. I felt a lightness in my heart that I had never felt before. It was OK to be me. I finally grasped the words of I John 3:1: "See what love the Father has given us, that we should be called children of God; and so we are." I fully understood what it meant to be "created in the image and likeness of God." I was that lost sheep that Jesus embraced. I was the prodigal son who made it home to an unexpected warm welcome. I felt that I could succeed and do some good things. For the first time in my life I felt that I was good enough for God just the way I was. This experience was the beginning of a new way of preaching. Instead of looking for sins to condemn, I started looking for goodness to affirm. I believe that the years following the dream prepared me to offer a clear message of "good news" that appealed to so many alienated Catholics which led to the rapid and consistent growth of the Cathedral parish a few years later.

## Calvary

In the fall of 1979, I was getting ready to end my first ten years of priesthood serving in the "home missions" of our diocese. It had been an intense ten years of personal growth and rather difficult ministry for a young priest in those days. I was not unhappy, but maybe I had the feeling that I had contributed what I could and that it was time for a change. Instead of waiting for the diocese to reassign me to a new parish, I asked to move into a whole new world.

I heard that a position at small parish in central Kentucky was going to be opening up with the retirement of its pastor. I applied and was offered the pastorate at Holy Name of Mary Church in Calvary, Kentucky, in what is called the "Catholic Holy Land" of central Kentucky – so called because it was where the first Catholics in the area settled and established churches. These parishes had long histories and traditions. In January of 1980, I found myself leaving one of the least Catholic areas of the state and one of the diocese's newest parishes to go to one of its oldest parishes in one of its most Catholic areas. Holy Name of Mary Church was founded in 1798. My ministry was about to change from serving a minority religion to serving a majority religion. It was the polar opposite of what I had just experienced.

My time as pastor of Holy Name Church was a time of great comfort. The people were so welcoming, so receptive and appreciative. In three and a half years we were able to clean up two cemeteries that had been neglected for years (one dating back to the late 1700s). We were also able to clean up a piece of property across the road from the church that had been left to grow up in weeds and small trees and turn it into a "park." We finished remodeling the old school/convent into a "retreat center." We were also able to repair and update the church and rectory. We did all this without one single "money talk" in church on Sundays.

In many ways, it was too easy and a time of calm before a storm of growth opportunities awaiting me in Louisville. It was there that I learned about the addictive power of comfort. I loved those people and they loved me. Our warm relationship continues to this day. I thought I would be there for a ten-year term. However, exactly three years into that assignment, the new Archbishop of Louisville, Thomas C. Kelly OP, had other plans. He called me one day and asked if I would come to Louisville to be pastor at the Cathedral of the Assumption. New to Louisville, he wanted to "do something" with the declining Cathedral parish and my name "kept coming up" when he talked about it to his advisors. He mentioned my Presbyterian Doctorate in Parish Revitalization. I had obviously made a name for myself in what I had accomplished in Monticello.

I was shocked by his request on many fronts. First, I was born in the country and I had never served as a priest in a city parish. Secondly, Archbishop Kelly wanted to sell his suburban residence and move in with me at the Cathedral rectory. Closeness to authority figures was an issue in my life at that time because of the history of my relationship with my father. Thirdly, I was only thirty-nine years old and the pastorate of the Cathedral were traditionally given to well-seasoned, senior clergy. Fourthly, the expectations of successfully reviving a center city parish were almost unrealistic to even think about. Some were even advocating putting the Cathedral on the list of parishes to be closed and making a suburban parish, Holy Spirit Church, our Cathedral.

The comfort of my nice little country parish took a hit the day of that phone call and the invitation from Archbishop Kelly. He gave me a few days to "think about it." My initial instinct was to say "no," but it became clear very quickly that he had "ruined" my comfortable assignment because if I were to turn it down, I would spend the rest of my life wondering "what if?" I knew I had to accept that assignment no matter how intimidating it appeared to be. My life up to that point had taught me that I "must" choose to do this hard thing for my own good. I knew in my heart of hearts that saying "yes" to this invitation would be monumental when it came to personal and spiritual growth. My instincts were right. I learned that all my small difficult choices were trial runs for the assignment ahead of me. I had no idea, really, how many more serious opportunities for growth and change I would be facing in the next several years.

Looking back, several things occur to me about those years in Calvary and Monticello before that. I was there to learn what I needed to learn for my next assignment at the Cathedral in Louisville. I learned about and gained an appreciation for the Catholic history of Kentucky. I was given an opportunity to learn what would later be called "the new evangelization" by Pope John Paul II. I learned how to be a missionary to the unchurched in preparation for going to a place to learn how to be a missionary to life-time

Catholics. I went to Monticello where I learned how to start a parish and then found myself in Calvary where I would learn how to revitalize a parish.

## The Cathedral

I arrived as pastor to the Cathedral in June of 1983. Archbishop Kelly, as a sign of his seriousness about my "doing something with it," moved five resident priests out on the same day, then sold his residence in the suburbs and moved into the Cathedral rectory with me in September of that year as a dramatic show of support.

Before I even unpacked, having heard from the former pastor that "nothing can be done at the Cathedral because there are no Catholics living downtown anymore," I took a folding lawn chair, went across the street and sat in the little Founders Square park and faced the Cathedral. I knew there were few people living downtown at that time, but I saw streets teaming with people moving about. I saw high rise office buildings full of people. I saw hotels and hospitals, restaurants and art centers, street people and tourists. Sitting there for a couple of hours, taking it all in, it occurred to me that half of those people were probably Catholic and more than half of those no longer went to church. All of a sudden, as if I were having another of the famous "Fourth and Walnut Thomas Merton experiences," my mission and purpose started to come into focus. I would try to get the half that no longer went to church, and those who had no church at all, to become the new Cathedral congregation. I realized that I would need to, once again, be an evangelist before I could be a pastor. I would have to preach a message that drew people in, a message of inclusion, hope and mercy. I saw great possibilities for parish revitalization and I was, thankfully so, blind at that time to the deteriorating condition of the Cathedral buildings.

My youth and inexperience may not have phased Archbishop Kelly, but it did his Auxiliary Bishop, Charles G. Maloney, who was in charge of diocesan finances. After months of trying to find out how much money the Cathedral parish had in reserves at the Chancery, Archbishop Kelly had to force Bishop Maloney to tell me. It was as if he thought, because of my age and inexperience, I would "run through" the savings in no time, leaving the Cathedral coffers empty. Even after being told to tell me how much savings the Cathedral parish had, he would dole out information a little at a time. I eventually found a file listing another account at the Chancery he had not told me about. Under the pressure of "doing something with the Cathedral," not being trusted with vital financial information and having my ideas for fund-raising being blocked, I finally reached a boiling point two years later.

I was not about to have my hands tied behind my back and be labeled a failure (my biggest fear) in carrying out the mission given to me, a mission I had not sought, because of one person's lack of trust in my judgement and ability. I knew it was a time to stand up for myself and "claim my power," so I decided to do something quite dramatic. I wrote a letter to Archbishop Kelly and copied Bishop Maloney. In it, I offered to either resign or be given some kind of public release from any serious expectation of ever "doing something with the Cathedral." Back then, that move might have been seen by some as youthful foolhardiness and by others as courage, but it worked. Throwing down the gauntlet resulted in the development of the path that would lead to dramatic, successful new growth for the Cathedral, it's parishioners and for me personally. I had seized the opportunity to stand up for myself before authority figures, something that had been an issue since childhood.

Several weeks after my offer to resign, I was told that Mr. Monty Shircliffe who was working in the Chancery Finance Department had been asked to work with me to set up a Development Committee for the Cathedral. In 1985, after the initial core team was assembled, including a long-time supporter of the Cathedral, Mr. Bert Paradis, other community leaders were asked to join. One of the great "finds" was Mrs. Christy Brown, wife of Owsley Brown, family CEO of Brown-Foreman Distillery, who still generously supports the ongoing efforts of the Cathedral. She not only became a co-worker but a good friend. She was yet another remarkable person I would meet because of my decision to leave Calvary and become pastor of the Cathedral.

Besides focusing on strengthening our liturgical programs of preaching, music and hospitality, the Cathedral Parish had set up special funds to receive financial gifts for ministries to the elderly and street people, and the arts and education programs we hoped to develop. We were already sponsoring a few concerts and guest speakers and expanding the ministry to street people from a food kitchen program to help with housing, clothing, counseling and job searches. We were also expanding ecumenical programs, especially through the existing Covenant with Christ Church Episcopal Cathedral.

Even before I arrived at the Cathedral, I was reading about the role of a Cathedral. I learned that it was three-fold. It had a ministry as the ceremonial church of the diocese. It was an independent parish in its own right. It had a significant role of service to the broader community. With the new Development Committee in place, it was decided that the Cathedral Parish would continue to focus on parish revitalization: especially liturgy, religious education and ministry to the elderly, while the Development Committee would take over the funds for the arts and street ministry and be responsible for the renovation and expansion of the facilities.

Unlike a medieval Cathedral in a "Catholic city," Cathedrals today are usually situated in a multi-religion community. Our outreach going forward should and would be ecumenical and interfaith. With that in mind, we chose the name "Cathedral Heritage Foundation" for the new development organization. I became the first president of the Foundation and Christy Brown its first vice president. What funds the parish had collected in special accounts for the arts and street ministry was turned over to the Cathedral Heritage Foundation. It was a win-win situation for the Cathedral parish. The Cathedral Heritage Foundation would develop the outreach programs to the community at large and take on the job of rehabilitating and renovating the property, while the parish could focus on the revitalization of the parish. I especially liked this arrangement because I had insisted that we not raise a huge amount of money to build a museum to 19th century Catholicism, but rather renovate those historic structures so that we could revitalize all three of the historic ministries of the Cathedral for today and into the future.

The parish grew from about 110 members to over 2100 members in fourteen years. The Cathedral Heritage Foundation raised over $26,000,000 to renovate and restore the Cathedral buildings, add much needed new space to the property and expand parish outreach. One of the most amazing aspects of the restoration of the Cathedral church was the lack of resistance from people and groups in the archdiocese and the community at large. I believe that it was because we were "going in the right direction." The gutting of the Cathedral during its previous "renovation" in the 1970s was considered by most people as an ill-advised loss of the building's integrity and a turning of its back on its own history. Once they understood that this new effort would wed the "best of the old and the best of the new," they were more than willing to support it financially. Once the community understood that it would be used by the whole community, in traditional cathedral fashion, the community stepped forward as well. For example, one bank gave $500,000 toward the restoration of the steeple and another company gave $1,000,000 toward the building of the dining room for the homeless. The only real problem that had to be solved was that a few Catholics had the mistaken impression that we were turning it into an "ecumenical cathedral." Once they understood that the outreach to the whole community has always been a "traditional cathedral ministry" and once firm boundaries were established between its three "missions," the vision was accepted.

During those years, I was being personally transformed as well. Almost weekly, I was faced with choosing to grow into my new role by standing up to my innate bashfulness and fear of meeting new people. I was rubbing elbows with politicians, playwrights, mayors, governors, national and local architects, leaders in the arts community, highly placed business leaders and religious leaders of multiple faiths including the Dalai Lama! I was interviewed regularly by TV, radio and print personalities, including one from Los Angeles. From the beginning, there were regular front pages stories about my time as pastor in the local newspaper and magazines. I had TV cameras show up for soundbites whenever anything happened locally or nationally about religion. I was being invited to speak at national conventions like the National Federation of Priest Councils and the new national Catholic Cathedral Convention.

Probably one of the most life-changing opportunities to develop another side of myself came with the opportunity to publish my first book. I woke up every morning during those years listening to a home-made "affirmation tape" I had made to encourage myself. People had been telling me for some time that my homilies "ought to be published." I did create some home-made tapes with several theme-based homily collections and made them available for sale in the Cathedral Heritage Foundation gift shop, but I was not yet convinced that they would have a broader than local appeal. I kept putting people off by saying, "I would, if I had an editor." For years that "affirmation tape" had one important "affirmation" in particular. Every morning, in my own voice, I heard myself say, "I am a published spiritual writer."

One day, on the steps of the Cathedral, a man said to me, "You ought to be publishing your homilies." I answered, "I would if I had an editor!" His response was, "I am an editor for Crossroads Press in New York, send me a manuscript." The challenge scared me to death, but I decided to stand up to my fear. I turned in my first manuscript, *An Encouraging Word: Renewed Hearts, Renewed Church*, and they published it. I still remember when the boxes of books arrived at the Cathedral rectory. I put them in my room, but I dreaded opening them. I let the boxes lay there on the floor until the next day before opening them. My fear of rejection, ridicule and judgment went into high gear because I was not confident yet that publishing a book was something I could or should do. Thank God I had the guts not to give in to that fear because this is actually my 34th book!

Another opportunity presented itself during those years. One of our local priests, Father Bill Griner, asked me to do a "parish mission," a three-night preaching event, in his parish. Again, I had to face my fear and choose courage over cowardice. The whole idea was daunting. I had never done a parish mission before. It meant that I would have to commit to a three-night, optional attendance speaking engagement, without knowing whether anyone would come to the first night, much less come the next two nights. At last count, I have conducted over 68 of them in three states, something that prepared me for the more than one hundred priest retreats in ten countries that would come later. I am still doing both.

## The Reconciliation

Growing up, I absolutely hated my father. I could not forgive him for the way he treated my mother, my siblings and me. I carried a festering rage for him for so long that I presumed it would be with me for the rest of my life. I was eaten up with anger, but something happened that year. I had just turned thirty-seven. I made one of the most important personal and most difficult decisions of my life, a decision that affected my life in a most positive way. It was most surely a moment of grace, a spontaneous gift from God.

My father was not the only guilty one in this drama. I had to admit, finally, that taking offense was just as destructive as the offense I was given. I got very good at passive-aggressive behaviors toward him: mumbling, gossiping and even sabotage. The acid of taking offense was eating me alive and my anger was doing more damage to me than to him. To get even, I would write home from the seminary to my mother and never even put his name on the envelop. I would call home when I knew he was not going to be there, and if he was there, I would never ask to speak to him or even tell him hello.

Mark Twain said something about anger that resonated with me more than anything I ever I have ever read. He said, "Anger is an acid that can do more harm to the vessel in which it is stored than to anything on which it is poured." One day, by the grace of God, I decided that I would have to find a way to forgive him or at least minimally let go of my obsessive negative thinking about him. I needed to do it for my own well-being. I certainly did not want him to die leaving me with unresolved issues that would rule my heart and mind for the rest of my life. At Mass, the words of the Our Father, "forgive us as we forgive those who trespass against us," would stick in my throat. I was telling people in Confession that they needed to forgive, but I couldn't! I started to believe what I had read somewhere, "To forgive is to set a prisoner free and discover that the prisoner was you." I prayed for months for God to change my heart. I set up an appointment with him twice and backed out.

Then one day I set up an appointment with him and it happened - at 6:30 pm, June 6, 1987. To my own surprise, I did not let him have it with both barrels as I had imagined I would do all of my life, but instead I forgave him and, shock of all shocks, I asked for his forgiveness for my retaliations to his meanness. It was certainly not an easy thing to do. It may have been the hardest thing I have ever done in my life. I prayed a long time for the strength and the opportunity to find healing. I felt as light as air on my

60

way home that night. We never spoke of it again. We never became friends, but I hugged him for the first and last time in my life as I left there. I was content just to be free of all that destructive hatred and anger. I can look at his grave today without one bit of resentment and with a lot of gratitude. I still wonder what my life would be like today if God had not helped me look at him with different eyes, if I had not wanted those different eyes or if he had died before I received that new way of seeing. I could still be imprisoned under the spell of resentment. Now I am free and so is he. Nothing changed but my mind – the way I chose to see things - and that has made a world of difference in my life.

One of the things I have come to realize of late is that his anger may have come from feelings of being trapped and held back by his growing family and its obligations. He always valued advanced education. He even served on the local County School Board. I think he always regretted not being able to continue in college (for reasons unknown to me) after his first semester at the University of Kentucky. He may have been carrying a lot of unresolved frustration that stemmed from a deep-seated regret that he had missed his own big "moment of grace." People often project their own issues onto others as a coping mechanism. We often do not know why people are like they are - what emotional traumas or life events they experienced that shaped their lives for better or worse.

People say that you cannot change the past, but you can. You can change the past by changing how you choose to remember it. You can change the past by looking at it from another point of view. You can change the past by moving from your own point of view to a new viewing point. From there you can appreciate, not only your own point of view, but other points of view as well.

## The Cathedral, Continued

Going into the renovation and restoration of the Cathedral, I was adamant about one thing. I did not want to be part of spending millions of dollars on preserving a museum to 19th century Catholicism. I wanted a strong living, breathing community of today's Catholics willing to carry on the traditional cathedral ministries in today's world. To build such a community, I knew that I had to either steal Catholics out of other parishes, convert great numbers of downtown workers to Catholicism or attract "fallen away" and "disaffected" Catholics who worked downtown. I had decided from day-one to focus on the latter.

From what I had learned from my Presbyterian Doctor of Ministry degree, I knew that the path forward involved "spending our time on preaching and hospitality and our money on music." I also knew intuitively that once we got a reputation for preaching, hospitality and music, they would ask for education. It worked. Month after month we grew by word of mouth, without any budget for advertising. We had such a reputation for welcoming disaffected Catholics that we earned the name of the "Island of Misfit Toys," from the kids TV Christmas Special, "Rudolph the Red-nosed Reindeer." I was not familiar with the story, so I rented the video. The "Island of Misfit Toys" was a special place where broken toys could go to be repaired so they too could be part of Christmas. The parish was honored by that nickname. In time, the crowds grew so large, especially at the Christmas Masses, that the Fire Marshall threatened to shut us down if we did not restrict the number of people in the building at one time. We even had to ask people to stop applauding at the end of homilies.

However, not everyone was happy about our new growth. A group of traditionalist Catholics were not happy about our welcoming of people from the margins, especially divorced, gay and lesbian Catholics. Two scary things in particular happened during those years. First, I had a knife pulled on me in the Cathedral itself over a homily welcoming marginal Catholics. Second, an anonymous "white paper" circulated in the community supposedly documenting mine and Archbishop Kelly's violations of Catholic Church teachings. In time, we ignored both and kept going. We knew that "all are welcome" did not mean "anything goes."

Another alarming event that occurred during those years is worth noting. At some point in the renovation and expansion of the facilities, digging around the foundation of the old 1852 building was required. Due to a miscommunication between the architect, the engineers and the construction company, multiple holes were dug under the old foundation all at the same time, rather than in progression over time. This caused the old building to start cracking down the apse's back wall and one side. I remember clearly standing out on the sidewalk watching and hearing it crack, believing that any moment the whole building would fall into a pile of rubble and somehow it happened on my watch! I heard my Dad's voice saying, "See! I told you that you would screw it up! Then I remember hearing my own voice, "You don't have the luxury of falling apart. You will be pastor of that parish next weekend whether that building falls down or not. Now get a grip!"

Like many other "breakdowns" in my life, this event actually turned out to be another "breakthrough." The whole community went in high gear to help us save the building. We were on the news three or four times a day for a month or two telling the people about the history of the building and what we had set out to do. Resources poured in. The parish continued to grow and the Cathedral Foundation became more and more visible in, and more attractive to, the community.

By 1997 the Cathedral renovations were finished and the parish was well on its way to revitalization. I was in my fourteenth year as pastor – four years longer than the term other pastors in the diocese were allowed to have. Archbishop Kelly told me that I could "stay as long as I wanted because he considered the Cathedral pastorate a personal decision of the bishop." Instead of hanging on, I knew in my heart of hearts, that it was time for me, once again, to "induce labor" in order to trigger another growth period. I told people that I was "good at hacking through the jungle and setting up the town, but other priests would make a better mayor." I made an appointment to see the archbishop and asked him if I could resign and receive another appointment. He accepted, but when I left his office and got into my car I felt that I had just committed a kind of personal "suicide" but I also knew it was the right thing to do. I had always asked the Cathedral congregation, "Who said you only get one golden age? I am here with you to be part of a new golden age." By that I meant that the Cathedral had once been a vibrant place and could be again if enough of us believed it. What is "good for the goose is good for the gander." In my own mind, it was very clear that I did not want to spend the rest of my life talking about my "Cathedral days." I was ready for another personal golden age and the only way it could happen was to move on. I knew I would have to go through a painful period of letting go.

After I left, the Cathedral Heritage Foundation changed its name to the Center for Interfaith Relations to more reflect its post-renovation period mission. It is still offering programs each year including its highly successful Festival of Faiths, which will celebrate its 24th year in April 2019. The Cathedral parish has seen its third pastor after me, and even though it went through a short period of shrinking again, it is now growing again and is about to launch a major campaign to create an endowment for long-term care of its buildings and the continuance of its vital programs. After twenty years of being away, I am now back helping out with Sunday Masses and serving as an "honorary chairman" for the new fund-raising campaign with my friend Christy Brown.

I took a six-month sabbatical after I left the Cathedral. Knowing myself, I remember telling Archbishop Kelly that I did not want to know what I would be doing next until I had some rest, otherwise I would start planning my next job. The sabbatical must have worked for this "workaholic" because I cannot remember, for the life of me, what I did for those six months other than take my dream cruise through the Greek islands.!

## Director of Vocations

By the end of my sabbatical, it was clear that Archbishop Kelly was thinking of offering me, as a "reward," one of the "plum parishes" of the diocese. I stopped him and asked, "After all this time, you still do not know me? Instead of one of the thriving parishes, give me two or three parishes about to close or the job of Vocation Director. I always do better in challenging situations!" I have always been more like Saint Paul, the patron of missionaries, than Saint Peter the patron saint of the established church. He gave me the job of Vocation Director. I left the Cathedral in June of 1997 and began my work as Vocation Director in January of 1998.

## Campus Ministry

The President of Bellarmine University was a parishioner at the Cathedral during my early years there. One day he said to me, "Someday you will be working at Bellarmine." I laughed it off as something that had never crossed my mind. However, by the fall of 1999, Bellarmine University was looking for a new Campus Minister and came knocking at my door. Since it seemed to fit hand in glove with the job of Vocation Director, I accepted. It was an opportunity to connect vocation recruitment to a regular exposure to a large number of young Catholic men and women. I did not need a second job, but Archbishop Kelly told me that he had no problem with my accepting the position, but he wanted to be clear that it was not an official assignment. He did not want the responsibility of trying to find a replacement when I left.

I was Campus Minister at Bellarmine University for seventeen years, twelve years longer than my job as Vocation Director. In that job I not only got to preside and preach at Sunday night Masses, but at annual Baccalaureate Masses in front of a church full of graduates, faculty, staff, parents and guests. To carry my preaching message to an even larger audience, I wrote three more books.

## The Sexual Abuse Scandal

During my tenure as a Vocation Director and a University campus minister, the priests sexual abuse scandal hit Louisville. Priests and their crimes, both local and national, were in the newspapers and on the evening news every day. During the peak, one of my best priest friends was dismissed from ministry. I was devastated for days. I was conflicted. I was frightened, ashamed, angry and filled with compassion, all at the same time. I felt a great need to do something, say something about how all of it was affecting me and likely my fellow priests. I submitted an article to *America*, a Catholic magazine, about my feelings. I wrote it on my front porch in less than an hour. It was entitled "Collateral Damage: How One Priest Feels These Days." I described some of my shame-filled behaviors, like putting my hand over my collar at stop lights. I talked about the "good side" of the priests I knew who were involved. I talked about my fear of being falsely accused of abuse. I talked about the support I was receiving from people in the pews. The article was published right away and I received affirmations from around the country from priests and parishioners alike who appreciated knowing how priests, not involved, were being affected.

## An Encouraging Word

In the fall of 2002, I was missing my Cathedral pulpit and it was painfully obvious to me that nobody seemed to be addressing the needs and fears of the average Catholic in the pew as the sexual abuse scandal raged. All the talk was about perpetrators, victims, lawyers and settlements. I wanted to do something to uplift and steady the faithful in those trying times. I asked the editor of *The Record*, the local Archdiocesan weekly newspaper, if I might try my hand at a weekly column to be called *An Encouraging Word*. I had no idea how long I would be writing that column. To my delight and my surprise, it became very popular. I wrote weekly for 15 years and finally decided to stop of my own choice in the fall of 2017. I found that very difficult even though I had started my own blog in August of 2015 also called An Encouraging Word. The blog provided me an avenue to stay connected to my faithful and appreciative readers by sharing homilies, personal insights and information about how they could be involved in my new volunteer work in the Caribbean missions.

From the beginning of my tenure as Vocation Director, I was collecting ideas on how to promote religious vocations in the Archdiocese of Louisville. I even wrote two books; one about diocesan priesthood and one about religious life. I was up to 17 ideas, but because everyone in the diocese seemed consumed and distracted by the sexual abuse scandal, I could not convince anyone to take them seriously. My frustration reached the boiling point during an inter-agency council meeting in the Chancery. At one point, I was practically screaming, "I don't mind being beat out by a better idea, but I am tired of being beat out by no ideas."

I went home, sat down at my computer with my finger on the "delete" button to rid myself of all seventeen ideas. At the very last minute, I pulled my finger back and said to myself, "No! These ideas are good. I think I should take these 17 ideas, put them in a book and offer a copy to every bishop in the United States." I asked to resign as Vocation Director and took a three-month sabbatical to refresh myself and work on a book that would eventually be titled *Intentional Presbyterates: Claiming Our Common Sense of Purpose as Diocesan Priests.* This little book propelled me into another "golden age." It was a hit nationally. Bishops were buying multiple copies as gifts to their priests. I had 7,000 copies in my garage at one time. I sold all of them and had it reprinted multiple times. Since then, I wrote a workbook to go with it and a follow-up book: *A Bishop and His Priests Together: Resources for Building a More Intentional Presbyterate.* I sent free copies of this book to all the bishops of the United States, Canada, England, Australia and South Africa.

## Institute for Priests and Presbyterates

Toward the end of my tenure as Vocation Director, I was invited to speak to the whole community of monks at Saint Meinrad Archabbey. Many of them had taught me in their seminary. I could talk about anything of my choosing. I remember thinking of all the reasons not to accept, but I eventually decided to do it. My topic was "A Modest Proposal: Seminary is No Longer Enough." I laid out the case for establishing an ongoing formation program for priests from ordination through retirement that would be just as serious and just as structured as the initial formation of seminary. The response was very positive, but I was told that they had no financing for such a serious venture.

About a year later, at the end of a faculty evaluation of one of our Louisville seminarians and knowing that I would be leaving my job as Vocation Director, I stayed behind and asked the Rector of the seminary, "Why don't you hire me to implement those ideas I talked about?" Oddly enough, just weeks later the Lilly Foundation in Indianapolis announced their "Making Connections" grants. The Rector suggested that we present my idea to them. We were given a $60,000 grant to write the proposal in detail. A few months later, we were given a full grant of $1,700,000 to implement the program.

From 2004 to 2013, I led what became known as the Saint Meinrad Institute for Priests and Presbyterates which has continued to flourish to this day. We initially began by focusing on priests in their first five years, but quickly expanded into transition out of the seminary, settling into priesthood, gearing up to be a pastor, acclimating international priests to American culture, presbyteral unity convocations, sabbaticals and finally a retirement program. Its focus is on individual ongoing formation and the ongoing formation of presbyterates in their unity. That program led to me being invited to direct well over 100 presbyteral unity convocations in ten countries. In retirement, I am still doing about six or so a year.

During those years, I wrote four more books for seminarians and priests. My growing reputation for being able to talk about presbyteral theology, in particular, led to my being invited to lead a seminary retreat in Texas and to deliver addresses at major Annual Lectures at seminaries in Wisconsin, Ohio and Missouri. It also led to the opportunity to address the American bishops as a body at the USCCB annual spring meeting in Florida and the USCCB member bishops of the Catholic Extension Society in Chicago.

While at St. Meinrad I also spearheaded four projects. I raised money to renovate a space into a coffee shop for students faculty, monks and staff. Computers and cell phones, we found out, were causing seminarians to stay in their rooms to do homework and text each other in the next room. The coffee shop gave them an inviting place to work together on projects and an opportunity to mingle with visitors, monks from the monastery, staff members and fellow seminarians. Because priests are increasingly living alone in a rectory I found resources to create a teaching kitchen that helps priests learn how to cook for themselves and collaborated with Tim Schoenbachler on a cookbook, *Daily Bread*, to be used as a textbook. To assist our new program for retired priests, I raised money to renovate a dorm wing into nice accommodations for program participants. From the monies that I had earned doing presbyteral retreats and convocations, I established a $100,000 endowment to teach parish revitalization. In 2010 I received an Alumnus of the Year award from St. Meinrad, but I felt they were more deserving of an award because they had nurtured this shy, fearful boy and enabled him to face life with confident boldness.

Toward the end of my years as a staff member of Saint Meinrad Seminary, I received a surprise invitation from Archabbot Justin to lead the annual monastic community retreat. I balked saying, "Archabbot, I know you guys too well!" He responded, "That's the point!" I cautiously agreed. It was a great success. That monastic retreat led to an invitation a second monastic retreat at Saint Benedict Abbey in Kansas later that year and a third monastic retreat for the Discalced Carmelite Community in Dallas in the fall of 2016. That initial decision led me to experience a world that I had only observed from a distance – the inner workings of monasteries.

In 2015, I turned 70. I was working on a retired priests program at St. Meinrad and recruited a pre-retirement specialist to teach pre-retirement planning. With the approval of the seminary Rector, I proposed to retire and to work on post-retirement programs from Louisville so as to give my successor room to breathe and time to learn the many other programs.

All was in place for a smooth transition – that is until my first meeting with my successor. Our first meeting lasted ten minutes. When I was explaining what the Rector and I had agreed to, he practically came across the table at me screaming, "I'm in charge now! I will decide what is done."

71

I stood up, walked out and went to the Rector's office. Even though he was willing to "work on it," I decided after much thought that it was not going to work and that I should bow out of a bad situation - some battles cannot be won – and so I fully retired from the program.

That was one of the most tumultuous eras of my ministry, mainly because it came about so suddenly and I had become so attached to implementing the retirement program as the capstone to years of post-seminary ongoing formation work. My head was filled with conflicting emotions. I had never been "fired," even though it felt like it. I had never been a "quitter." I never felt so betrayed. I was having a hard time "letting go" of one of my dreams and feeling powerless to do anything about it.

When the walls of the Cathedral cracked during the renovation process, I learned that the turning point at which you begin to attain success is usually defined by some point of defeat or failure. I learned that one need not accept defeat as a failure, but only a temporary event that may prove to be a blessing in disguise. Defeat is never the same as failure unless and until it is accepted as such.

After several months I decided to start my own experiential retirement program for retiring priests, bishops and lay professionals. I called it the Catholic Second Wind Guild. It has two Chapters – one in Saint Vincent and the Grenadines and one in Barbados. My dream is to have another Chapter in Alaska someday. The purpose, as I envisioned it, was to offer retiring priests, bishops and lay professions a structured way to offer their services in new and interesting ways to areas of the church in desperate need of such services. My idea was that it would be good, both for those volunteering, and for the places where their services were needed.

Retirement from Saint Meinrad Seminary left me completely free to develop the Catholic Second Wind Guild on my own. In its fourth year, it is going even better than I had predicted. I completed my tenth trip down there in June of 2018. It is so true that when one door closes, another opens. In this case, several new doors have opened.

During all of those years, the practice of responding to moments of grace and the benefits that came from it, were happening regularly. Looking back, it seems that the decisions that led up to these years were only a "warm up for the big race." Truly, when we face our fears and really commit to something worthwhile then Providence moves too. All kinds of unforeseen incidents, meeting new people, offers of financial assistance from generous donors for projects manifested themselves. As I think back over these years, I become very aware that I could have missed all of it by giving into fear and laziness, simply saying "no" to God's grace and settling for too little.

# MY SECOND WIND

Les Brown, American motivational speaker, wrote, "You are never too old to set another goal or to dream a new dream." I went into "retirement" with some pretty strong feelings about reinventing myself once again. I was asking myself, "Why can't the days ahead be the good old days? Why would you want to sit around and bore people with your reminiscing about the days gone by? I knew I wanted to "do" retirement differently than our culture presents it - a time to slow down, to pamper oneself and to be taken care of. I wanted to look at retirement as a time to get a check deposited in my bank account without having to report in. I wanted to live simply on Social Security, my diocesan retirement benefits and what I had saved, while continuing to work and earn money to give to my charities.

In preparation for retirement, I took a test called the Retirement Success Profile for Diocesan Priests. It measured fifteen things like whether I was financially, spiritually and emotionally prepared for retirement. I scored pretty high in most areas, but when it came to things like "leisure," I basically flunked.

People laughed when I told them I was retiring, so I made excuses like, "You have to bring the car to a slow stop. If you slam on the brakes, you might go through the windshield." Many people may look on this habit as something to be pitied, rather than be praised, but I have always marched to the sound of a different drummer and I feel no need to change just because I have reached my 70th birthday.

I may be, no, I am what you call a "workaholic." Another symptom is the fact that I had been working for Saint Meinrad Seminary for about six years before I realized that the word "vacation" was not even mentioned in my job description. It didn't even occur to me to ask. It wasn't until I went through my exit interview with the people down at human resources that I knew I was entitled to four weeks a year. I left with them owing me thirty-six weeks of vacation time!

Since I had learned first-hand, over many years of practice, the tremendous rewards of conscious deliberate growth, why would I "retire" from that? I knew I wanted to continue seeing how much further I could take myself with God's help. I knew that if I committed to that goal, Providence would move again, throwing all sorts of assistance and opportunities onto my path. I am still on the hunt for who I've not yet become.

I made a passionate commitment to keep looking for new experiences and new opportunities for personal growth in both of the two stages that lay in front of me: while I still have my health and even after my health begins to fade. "The last of the human freedoms," as Viktor Fankl said, "is the freedom to choose one's response to any given situation." Even when my mobility, sight and hearing fail, I believe there is always *something* I can do besides "give up!" Yes, I may need to work on a balance between work and rest, but I still don't want to "go gentle into that good night, but rage, rage against the closing of the day," as Dylan Thomas put it. No! George Bernard Shaw is the drummer I want to march to in my "senior" years. I can't repeat it enough. "This is the true joy in life, the being used for a purpose recognized by yourself as a mighty one; the being thoroughly worn out before you are thrown on the scrap heap; the being a force of Nature instead of a feverish selfish little clod of ailments and grievances complaining that the world will not devote itself to making you happy."

I retired from Saint Meinrad Seminary in 2013, the Archdiocese of Louisville in 2014 and Bellarmine University in 2016. I am "on my own" and love it. I joke with people that all my aggravations are now "self-inflicted." I don't *have* to do the things I do. If I do them, I do them because I *choose* to do them.

One critical event, however, happened in the early summer of 2014. It woke me up to the precariousness of old age. I had received a gift certificate for a month in a small castle in France as a retirement gift from a good friend who had bought it at a fund-raiser. Everything was ready to go. A friend and I had first class airplane tickets, train tickets and a rental car all lined up. A week before we were to leave, I noticed that my left leg appeared reddish for some reason. I went online to see what some of the symptoms might indicate, which is always a bad idea. Because I was going to be gone a month, I decided to go to the emergency room down the street and have it checked out, just in case. After four hours of waiting, I was so disgusted that I was seriously thinking of going home and forgetting about it. This was a time when "doing hard things for my own good" actually saved my life. I toughed it out and was seen by a doctor who told me that I had a blood clot and that I was going to be admitted right then and there. I was told not to move off the ER table or get out of bed for a week while I was pumped full of blood thinners to dissolve the clot. I was stunned to find out that if I had gotten on the plane, I would probably be dead before I got to France. After a week in the hospital, I came home and continued my retirement, happy that I had resisted the easy, but deadly, way.

During retirement, I have chosen to keep leading priest retreats all over the United States, Canada and the Caribbean. I don't advertise but I keep getting four or five invitations a year that I am more than willing to accept as my calendar permits. I continue to maintain my blog with posts every other day or so. I still accept invitations to do two or three "parish missions" around the diocese. I have been invited back to help with a Sunday Mass at the Cathedral every weekend where I used to be the pastor and where I have no need to be the "boss" anymore. I am like a grandfather, who can enjoy the grandkids and send them home after visiting with them for a few hours. I accept invitations to speak to various groups as they come in, especially those that propel me into scary new situations: The Canon Law Society of America, Notre Dame University's Marten Program in Homiletics and a priest and deacon retreat for the Eparchy of Parma, Ohio.

The most significant part of my retirement years, so far, has been my involvement in my two new organizations: R J Mission Projects and the Catholic Second Wind Guild. R J Mission Projects (R stands for Ron and J stands for Jim) was started while I was still working at Saint Meinrad Seminary. It initially was a fund that we started together to help international seminarians. R J Mission Projects continues even today with a new focus – the needs of the Caribbean missions and the renovation of the Monte Cassino Shrine and Prayer Garden at Saint Meinrad Archabbey.

While I was still Director of the Institute for Priests and Presbyterates, developing my plans for the pre-retirement program, I had the vision of finding interesting places for retired priests to volunteer – in a warm climate in the winter and a cold climate in the summer. I had no connections, but I was thinking of the Caribbean during the winter and Alaska during the summer months. I knew that both places had severe priest shortages, so it would be a win/win situation. The missions would get a "free" priest and the retired priests would get a "free" vacation.

Be careful what you pray for! One morning, very early, I was in the seminary dining room having coffee and waiting for breakfast to be served. The only other person there was a visiting bishop. I had heard that Bishop Jason Gordon was on campus visiting his seminarian. He was the world's only bishop of two dioceses in two countries at the same time: Barbados and Saint Vincent and the Grenadines. It was me and him. I almost panicked as my mind raced between introducing myself or letting him be. "What if he thinks I am crazy? What if he rejects my intrusion? What if he were to say "no" to my inquiry?"

Finally, giving into my fear, I took my coffee and left the dining room and started walking to my room. Half-way down the long hall, I said to myself, "Are you nuts? This is your opportunity! Go with the risky choice. Go back and ask him. You will never forgive yourself if you let this opportunity pass." I turned around, went back into the dining room, walked up to him and introduced myself. I told him that I was a retiring staff member of the continuing education department and that I was trying to develop a program whereby myself and other retired US priests might volunteer some of their time in the Caribbean missions. He grabbed me by both shoulders and said, "Yes! Yes! We can even present this idea to all the bishops of the Caribbean!" I was a bit shocked and said, "Well, let me come down and visit first. We will start in your two countries and then see where it goes." The rest of the story is history. In mid-June of 2018, I returned from my 10th trip down to Barbados and Saint Vincent and the Grenadines.

During those ten trips, a lot has happened. As I was planning my first trip down, Bishop Gordon suggested that I focus first of all on the country of Saint Vincent and the Grenadines (Diocese of Kingstown), a much poorer country than Barbados (Diocese of Bridgetown). My first trip was exploratory. On the next trips, I would fly from Louisville to Miami and on to Barbados. I would stay overnight with Bishop Gordon in Barbados and then fly on to Saint Vincent the next day and reverse the process on my way home.

Sometime after my third or fourth trip, at Bishop Gordon's request, a new bishop for the Diocese of Kingstown in SVG was named by Pope Francis. He is Bishop Gerard County. I remember Bishop Gordon telling me after that announcement, "I am not going to let you go. You still have to help me in the Diocese of Bridgetown, Barbados." After the appointment of Bishop County, Bishop Gordon was left to be the full-time Bishop of Bridgetown, Barbados. I led his priest retreat, helped him buy some TV recording and studio equipment for his evangelization program. We talked about the need for a new retreat house at some of his existing property and even started to draw up some initial plans.

During these early years, I was getting more and more involved in the Diocese of Kingstown SVG as he had recommended. I remember sitting on the patio of the Diocese of Kingstown Pastoral Centre with both bishops sometime during the episcopal ordination of Bishop County. I told them that if my program was going to work, we had to "do something" with the Pastoral Centre. It was not a place that was conducive to house retired US priests. It was badly in need of renovation – from plumbing to furniture. I suggested that the renovation of that space should be my first priority, even while we reached out to strengthen the ministries of the diocese: the poor, the schools, the orphanages, the diocesan offices and the ongoing formation of clergy and lay leadership.

The short of it is this. I led their priest retreat, introduced the idea of Catholic Second Wind Guild and secured their support of the idea. Since then I have led two deacon formation retreats, filled in at several parishes including Holy Week Services, baptized seven babies, visited the two orphanages twice, was interviewed on a local radio station, visited the Minster of Health in his office, preached at a Soup Kitchen service, toured some of the schools and established a kids' summer computer camp. The Catholic Second Wind Guild has recruited three professional level volunteers to assist the clergy and teach the children, as well as established a close working relationship with two full-time volunteers from Ireland. In between all this, I had the opportunity to teach seminarians in Trinidad, address the Antilles Bishops Conference and visit the Vatican Embassy in Port of Spain, Trinidad.

The biggest success so far is the almost complete renovation of the Diocese of Kingstown Pastoral Centre. Funds have already been collected for a new entrance and several ongoing programs, office equipment, kids Christmas parties on all the islands, toys and snacks for the orphanages, a 40 foot shipping container of surplus medical supplies for the islands hospital and clinics, tuition for one of the Sisters continuing education, clothes for kids, school supplies, a boat motor, the repair of the roof of Saint Joseph House on Union island, three vans and the bishop's car, several designated funds including a maintenance fund for the Pastoral Centre to name a few. The total funds raised is about 2,000,000 East Caribbean dollars (about 740,000 US dollars). All this was accomplished in just three years, thanks to the generosity and encouragement of so many friends in the Archdiocese of Louisville, R J Mission Projects and the many Dioceses who have given me generous stipends for leading their priest retreats.

As things have picked up in the Diocese of Kingstown SVG, it has slowed down in the Diocese of Bridgetown Barbados because Bishop Gordon has been promoted to Archbishop of Port of Spain, Trinidad. I have led the priest and deacon retreat in the country of Saint Lucia. The Catholic Second Wind Guild is morphing to adjust to these emerging realities, but the dedication to, and passion for, these ministries continue to evolve and expand. Now that the program is up and going, and now that we have a decent place to house volunteers, we hope to attract a more serious stream of clerical and professional lay volunteers coming down to help. We hope to develop more partnerships with schools and religious service agencies in the US and SVG. The stage is set for some serious growth and development.

It is not lost on me that all this is happening because I changed my mind, seized a moment of grace and went back to speak to Bishop Gordon that early morning in the cafeteria of Saint Meinrad Seminary six years ago. The words of Joseph Campbell are worth repeating, "The cave you fear to enter holds the treasure you seek."

# PRINCIPLES FOR BECOMING YOUR BEST SELF

## How Spiritual Growth Happens

When we are ready to stand up to our fear, and maybe even cowardice, and we are intent on deliberately choosing to do hard things for our own good, what can we expect? Positive responses to "moments of grace," invitations to change and growth, seem to have certain classic "movements:" an entry period, an exploration period and finally a validation period.

The best scriptural story to explain how personal growth happens, I believe, is the story of the Exodus. Exodus is the story of people being called to something new, setting out in excitement, being tempted in discouragement to back out of the process, the decision for fidelity and finally arriving at a new level of being.

### THE ENTRY PERIOD

The "entry period," the first stage of our own personal growth, could be anything that shakes our present world to its foundation. For me, it was that powerful new awareness of the possibility of a better life and my own willingness to show up and do the work of self-actualization.

For others, an entry event might be a heart attack, a divorce, a death, a serious illness, major surgery or sudden unemployment. The entry point might also be some unplanned encounter: a new book, an adult education course, a new acquaintance or maybe even a moving song or a great homily. If we embrace the experience, growth is possible. If we reject the experience, a little more of ourselves withers away.

These entry events remind me of the old cowboy movies when the bad guys are "holed up" in an old cabin. The good guys throw a rock through the window with a note, giving them their options, "Come out and live or stay in and die!" Our entry events can be understood as "rocks" that come crashing through the windows of our lives with this message attached to them: "Opportunity is knocking!"

There are numerous ways to respond to these surprise invitations that come crashing into our lives. Some people respond to their "entry events" with the curiosity of children. Unafraid, they reach out to inspect and explore them. This is the response Jesus advocates. "Unless you become like a child, you will not enter the reign of God."

I have, over the years, observed people who respond this way. They are the widows who have a good, long cry and then courageously set out to create a new life. They are the amputees who push themselves to compete in the Handicapped Olympics. They are the millions of AA members who celebrate their sobriety. One day a "rock" came crashing into their world and, somehow, they got that spark of courage necessary to say "yes" to its invitation to change and to stand up to all the "demons" who tried to dissuade them.

Another way to respond to such entry events is to run. Those who respond this way are often people who are afraid of having to let go of some favorite old habits, afraid of losing control, afraid of having to revise their maps of reality, afraid of all the work that real change will require of them. Instead of directing their energy into finding the opportunity inside this new situation, those who run from them waste their energy on resisting this unwanted reality. They think to themselves: "If I just don't like this enough, maybe it will go away." These are the people who go through life fine-tuning their impressive list of reasons for not being happy: "If this had not happened . . .," "if it weren't for him or her . . .," "if it weren't for the times we live in . . ." or "if I were just not a victim of circumstances."

One final way to respond to an entry events is to hesitate. Some people hesitate because of concern about how significant people in their lives might react should they seriously start to change. Sometimes this hesitation and lack of curiosity is used as a defense against fear. As much as we like to complain, often we don't really want things to be all that different. "What if I might have to become committed to some demanding discipline? What if I find out that what I really want out of life is radically different from what I have? What if I get "caught up" in something, start having weird new experiences, and worse yet, even like them?"

Somewhere at each entry point we are asked to decide between "yes" or "no" as to whether we are open to change or not. Even if we say "yes," those of us with second thoughts can say "no" and exit the process at any time. But if we do say "yes," and stick with it, then things will never be quite the same. We are on our way to becoming a new person.

## THE EXPLORATION PERIOD

We might call the second stage of personal transformation the "exploration period." After saying "yes" to an entry event that offers us an invitation to growth and change, we enter, either warily or enthusiastically, an exploratory phase. Having sensed there is something worth finding, we leave one shore and set sail for another. No longer resisting or fighting the process, our mind courageously opens up to receive something new. An open mind is essential before anything can change. With this new openness, the adventure of transformation begins.

In the exploratory period of personal growth, the seeker sooner or later gets a taste of the world to come and, liking the taste, becomes like a kid in a candy store. Like Peter in the Transfiguration gospel story, who has an intense religious experience, suggests putting up three tents and staying on the mountain forever, we want to make the taste of this new world to become permanent. The initial taste, the first success, is so empowering that we enter a period of "busy seeking." On one hand we experience exhilaration. We can't get enough of the new technique, teacher or program. We keep seeking to duplicate the initial, powerful experience. On the other hand, we also feel loneliness. In this phase, we can become obnoxious evangelists, driven to tell the whole world of their newly discovered cure for all ills. If people don't burn out during this stage, or drive others crazy, they are ready to go deeper. The essential thing in this stage is not to give up, but to graduate.

However, not too long into this period, "demons" jump around in our head or onto our path to frustrate our plan and trip us up. They try to make us lose sight of our goal or convince us that we have fallen into a hopeless situation. This is precisely where we all sink or swim in the transformation process. Just because things are not turning out just as we had planned does not mean we should give up. This simply forces us to turn to our creative source and find an alternative way to attain our goal. Frustration is a necessary component of any transformation process. Do not make the mistake of giving up on your aspiration if you encounter what appears to be an impasse. Your response to this imagined impasse is what is truly important.

Many exit the process here during the exploration process. That's what all that whining is about in the Exodus story. They want to back out of the process and go back to safety. "Why did you ever make us leave Egypt? Was it just to have us die here from thirst? At least we had plenty to eat in the old days." Abused women often return to their abusers at this point in the process. The "known" is not as scary as the "unknown."

If you expect such initial responses, face such situations and hold your ground, you will begin to see solutions you never thought of. Anyone going through the process of personal transformation finds themselves in the shoes of the Israelites at some point or another. Unfortunately, you may have to go through several of these episodes during this phase. This is the stage marked with dissonance, sharp conflict, oscillation and testing.

## THE VALIDATION PERIOD

Having triumphed over all the temptations to give up, go back and quit, another step opens up in the process. Breakthroughs and insights begin to happen to you and all around you. They might come with a jolt of amazement or a simple quiet knowing. Almost before you know it, you find that you are becoming the new person you set out to be. This is a period of new strength and sureness. This is the next step after all the messes, setbacks and frustration. You will finally understand that breakdowns are often the surest signs that breakthroughs are imminent. You will finally know that pain is not a good reason to exit the process. Rather, it can be the best reason to stay the course.

Once you have been through these "movements" a few times, you begin to understand how transformation works. You know you will inevitably have to go through an unsettling period of disillusionment temporarily throwing you into a bottomless pit. You learn to expect this and know that it is important to ride this period out, realizing that victory is also inevitable. Here, the words of the Prophet Habakkuk come to mind: "For the vision still has its time, presses on to fulfillment, and will not disappoint; if it delays, wait for it, it will surely come, it will not be late."

## THE REPETITION PERIOD

Having discovered how transformation works and having mastered the process, you are finally ready to start "throwing rocks through your own windows." You are ready to induce your own labor pains of growth and set out on one journey after another. You begin to deliberately choose to do hard things for your own good. You will understand that "moments of grace" keep coming and you can keep being transformed, over and over again, depending on how much courage you have and how intense your thirst is for being "created anew," as St. Paul called it.

In the previous pages I tracked my responses to my own "moments of grace." I hope they triggered memories in your own life when you have consciously or unconsciously responded to God's invitation to becoming all that you can be. Once you know that you have unconsciously responded, you can learn to respond consciously and have what Jesus called "life to the full."

# BECOMING YOUR OWN HERO

## Because There is No Rescue Party Out Looking for You

*A hero is someone who, in spite of weakness,*
*doubt or not always knowing the answers,*
*goes ahead and overcomes anyway.*
Christopher Reeve

One of the most enduring literary forms is the "quest" or the "hero's journey." The object of a "quest" requires great exertion on the part of the hero, the overcoming of many obstacles, typically including much travel into the land of tests and adventures. The hero normally aims to obtain something with the goal of returning home. The object of the journey can be a new insight, something that fulfills a lack in life, or something or someone who was stolen or abducted.

Examples from literature include Homer's *Odyssey*. After the fall of Troy Odysseus was cursed by the gods to wander and suffer for many years until Athena persuaded the Olympians to allow him to return home to his wife and son. Recovering the Golden Fleece is the object of the travels of Jason and the Argonauts in *Argonautica*. Many of us are familiar with the quest for the Holy Grail and the adventures of King Arthur, Guinevere and Sir Lancelot. Then there is the mock quest of Don Quixote, who nonetheless remains a hero of chivalry. (Who has not been to a high school graduation without having been challenged by "To Dream the Impossible Dream" from "Man of La Mancha?") Then there is the *Wizard of Oz*, where Dorothy, the Scarecrow, the Tin Man and the Cowardly Lion go on a quest for the way back to Kansas, for brains, for a heart and for courage.

The "quest" theme in literature continues into our own day. One of my favorite contemporary quest stories is "The Never Ending Story" about a young boy Bastian, who while reading a book, gets personally pulled into the heroic adventures of Atreyu on his heroic trip to Fantasia. Most young people today have grown up with Frodo's quest in *The Lord of the Rings* trilogy, a tale of friendship and inner struggle with temptation, against a background of epic and supernatural warfare.

From Scripture, the story of the Magi has all the qualities of a traditional "quest" story. There is risk, adventure, determination, long distance travel, tests, intrigue, diversions and finally a trip home. The Magi were priest-teachers to the kings of Persia, modern day Iraq. Their job was to watch the heavens for any unusual activity. Unusual activity among the stars was a sign that a great leader was being born and they were compelled to check it out. Astrologers today even know the name of the star they followed. It was called 'The Birth of a Prince Star." They left everything that was comfortable and familiar to them and set out to new lands, seeking new insights and new understanding. Their search led them to Jesus.

What has all this to do with us? Surely, we realize that we are not here to admire other people's adventures from history, literature or Scripture. We are here to be challenged by these heroes to go on our own personal quests. In fact, that is one of the weaknesses of today's culture. We would rather watch sports than play them; listen to music than learn to play an instrument or sing ourselves; play video games with imaginary heroes than attempt to become heroes ourselves.

A great template for a hero's journey, anyone on a quest to become someone new or to fulfill his or her dreams, is again, the Old Testament story of the Exodus. That pattern – setting out in enthusiasm, a period of testing and regret, a decision to go forward rather than go back and finally arriving at success is true whether you want to lose weight, leave a dysfunctional relationship or even graduate from college.

I adopted this template years ago and I have embraced it for my recent retirement. My worst nightmare was to go into retirement accepting the popular belief that it was a time to slow down, take care of myself and expect to be pampered by others. The rocking chair is a symbol of retirement in our country. I say "to hell" with rocking chairs! Get them out of my sight. I want to reinvent myself. I want a new adventure. I want to see how far I can push myself. I'm on the hunt for who I've not yet become. I want to create a life that still makes me want to jump out of the bed in the morning.

I just returned from my 10th trip to the island country of St. Vincent and the Grenadines, right off the coast of Venezuela. Here I am at 74, doing foreign missionary work, living in a foreign country, meeting people from other cultures and getting involved in projects I would never have imagined. I am a bit amazed at myself going through foreign airports by myself with a backpack and putting myself in some pretty scary situations. It is not easy, but for me it certainly more exciting than playing golf, puttering around the yard or just sitting around the pool. No matter what, I don't want to end up like the old woman from Eastern Kentucky who had never been more than two miles from the spot where she was born. When asked why she had never her whole life left the place where she was born, she answered, "I just don't believe in goin' places!" Life is about "going places."

"Start taking full responsibility for the quality of life you are living. Stop blaming the situations in your life and the people in your life for the troubles you are facing. The best day of your life is one when you decide your life is directly proportionate to your own action and decisions. The day you realize that no one is going to come and win your emotional battles for you will be the day you become a warrior. You will become your own hero." (Aarti Khurana)

Become your own hero. It begins with a changed mind and a new outlook.

"Whatever you can do or dream you can, begin it. Boldness has genius, power and magic in it. Begin it now." (Johann Wolfgang von Goethe)

# THE JONAH COMPLEX

## The Convenience of Playing Small

*You can run with the big dogs
or sit on the porch and bark.*
Wallace Arnold

In the first pages of the Book of Genesis, we are told that human beings are created in the image and likeness of God. This mystery both triggers fear and fascination causing us to attempt to be more than we are or less than we are, but not fully who we are. Again, Abraham Maslow was right, "We both crave and fear becoming truly ourselves."

Not knowing who we are is a very old problem. It goes all the way back to the story of Adam and Eve. According to that mythic story, at the end of creation God, humans and the animals lived in harmony. They were interconnected and interdependent. As a colorful Baptist preacher said at one of my graduations, "In the beginning, God was happy being God. The animals were happy being animals. Human beings, however, have never been happy being human beings. They've wanted to be God one day and animals the next!"

Because we are created in the image and likeness of God, we all have the chance to become our very best selves. We all feel something inside, a quiet "maybe" that is often silenced as quickly as it is surfaced. We enjoy and even thrill before the godlike possibilities we see in ourselves and simultaneously shiver with fear before these very same possibilities. As a result, the overwhelming majority of us fail to achieve a life even close to what we are capable of achieving. In face of our godlike possibilities, we let the fear of possibilities overpower the thrill of possibilities. Afraid of being different, afraid of being uncomfortable and unsafe, afraid of failure and ridicule, we give into our innate tendency towards mediocrity and conformity, even to the point of sabotaging our potential for the sake of comfort and safety. However, if we deliberately settle on being less than we are capable of being, we will be deeply unhappy for the rest of their lives. "The tragedy of life is not death . . . but what we let die inside of us while we live." (Norman Cousins)

I read recently that obesity is growing in our culture, but narcissism is grower even faster. Narcissism is the term used to describe excessive vanity and self-centeredness. The condition was named after a mythological Greek youth named Narcissus who became infatuated with his own reflection in a lake. He did not realize at first that it was his own reflection, but when he did, he died out of grief for having fallen in love with someone who did not exist outside himself.

Narcissistic personalities are characterized by unwarranted feelings of self-importance. They expect to be recognized as superior and special, without necessarily demonstrating superior accomplishments. They exhibit a sense of entitlement, demonstrate grandiosity in their beliefs and behaviors and display a strong need for admiration. Some believe inflated self-importance has led to a disdain for those they feel are inferior, which might explain a rise in bullying among the young.

When narcissistic people talk about church attendance, they usually say things like "I don't go because I don't get anything out of it!" "I, I, I!" When they say things like that they put themselves in the center of the picture. It's all about them! Church attendance is really about giving, not getting. We go to Church as God's people to give God thanks and praise and support one another in our faith. We go to learn about our mission to serve others.

When narcissistic people talk about marriage, they talk about what it will do for them. They are like the woman in the Guinness Book of Records with the most marriages. When she was asked about it, she said, "All I ever wanted was someone to love me." No wonder she failed at it so many times. People who marry successfully get married to be love-givers, not love-getters. As Jesus said, "It is in giving that one receives." Receiving is not a goal, but a by-product, of the marriage commitment.

When narcissistic diocesan priests talk, they tend to focus on what the Church owes them, focus on the imagined privileges other priests have that they don't have and even act out to stand out.

When narcissistic young people talk about what to do with their lives, they usually ask themselves "what do I want to do or what do I want to be" that will make me happy? The real question is not what do we want to do, but what is God calling me to do and be" that will lead me to happiness? Jesus said, "Those who seek to save their lives will lose them, while those who seek to give their lives away, will save them." Albert Schweitzer said, and narcissistic people will never get it, "The only ones among you who will be really happy are those who have sought and found out how to serve." Dr. Martin Luther King, Jr. said, and narcissistic people will never understand it, "Life's most persistent and urgent question is, "What are you doing for others?"

Pope Francis talks a lot about a "self-referential Church," in other words a narcissistic Church. He says that when the Church does not look beyond itself, when it is always focused on itself, it gets sick. The Church is the moon and Christ is the sun. The Church exists to reflect the light of Christ to the world, not to live within herself, of herself and for herself.

The other extreme to narcissism is self-deprecation or the minimization and devaluation of oneself. Humility is about accepting the truth about who we are, without exaggerating it or minimizing it. "Humility" comes from the Latin "humus," meaning "earth." "Humility" means "grounded." A truly "humble" person, truly in touch with his strengths and weaknesses, neither inflates his worth nor devalues it. Humility is ultimately about truth.

Jesus spent his ministry trying to teach this truth. He taught it to the religious leaders of his day who were so arrogant and self-inflated that they started out talking about God and ended up thinking they were gods. He taught it to the marginalized of his day who were so beaten down that they did not recognize their own goodness and the image of God within themselves. All this is summarized so well in the *Magnificat* when Mary talked about the "mighty being pulled from their thrones and the lowly being lifted up from their dunghills."

God has entrusted gifts to us to be used. When we do not use our gifts, even deny we have them, we neither serve God nor the people we are called to serve. Jesus told us that we are the light of the world, our light is not to be hidden, but shared with the world. When they are shared, the credit is not to be absorbed by us as if we were the source of that light, but that credit is to be reflected back to God. Seeing our light, people are to give God the glory and praise.

There is great responsibility that goes with being the light of the world and having talent. It scares us. We tend to shy away from it. Marianne Williamson summarized it best when she said:

"Our deepest fear is not that we are inadequate, our deepest fear is that we are powerful beyond measure. It is our light, not our darkness, that most frightens us. We ask ourselves, who am I to be brilliant, gorgeous, talented, and fabulous – actually, who are you not to be? You are a child of God. Your playing small doesn't serve the world. There is nothing enlightened about shrinking so that other people won't feel insecure around you. We were born to make manifest the glory of God within us. It is not just in some of us: it is in everyone, and as we let our own light shine, we unconsciously give other people permission to do the same."

This is why I love the story of that little sawed-off guy, Zacchaeus, in the Gospel of Luke. He wanted to get a glimpse of Jesus coming down the road, but he was too short to see above the crowd! He could have said, "Oh, well, maybe next time," but he didn't. He found an alternative. We are told that he "ran ahead" and "climbed a sycamore tree" alongside the road where Jesus would be passing by. Because of his ingenuity and determination, Zacchaeus not only got to see Jesus, but Jesus was able to see him in the tree and admiring his determination, invited himself to Zacchaeus' house for dinner.

Zacchaeus reminds me of those guys who wanted to get Jesus' attention in another gospel story. Their buddy needed healing. He was crippled. When the door of the house where Jesus was staying was blocked by huge crowds of people, they could have given up and carried him back home. Instead they carried him up on the roof, tore a hole big enough to lower their buddy down, right in front of Jesus! Jesus commended them for their determination and healed their crippled friend right then and there.

"It is our light, not our darkness, that most frightens us." Nothing stings like the realization of a missed opportunity, but what stings even more is the realization of a refused calling. In that arena, the Old Testament prophet, Jonah, is a patron saint. Jonah was called to preach to the people of Ninevah. He considered himself a poor preacher on one hand and the Ninevites not worth saving on the other. To get away from his unwelcomed call, he went down to the docks and bought a ticket on the next ship sailing in the opposite direction from Ninevah. He thought he could outrun God!

In his version of a get-away-car, Jonah is pictured going to sleep in the bottom of his boat while a storm raged, a symbol today of "denial." The psychologist Abraham Maslow calls such spiritual and emotional truancy the Jonah Complex: "The evasion of one's own growth, the setting of low levels of aspiration, the fear of doing what one is capable of doing, voluntary self-crippling, pseudo-stupidity, mock humility."

We are afraid of failure and success. A calling makes us wonder if we are good enough, smart enough, disciplined enough, educated enough, patient enough, and inspired enough. We manage our fear by "going to sleep," "settling for too little" and "self-sabotage." The truth is this: all of us have answered "yes" in some areas and "no" in others. We both crave and fear becoming who we are called to be.

It is true that narcissism, exaggerating our importance can be a problem, but so can the minimization of our importance. Maslow proposes that there is a cluster of fears underlying the fear of greatness that cause us to evade our true calling and instead adhere to the security of simply having undemanding goals instead of grand ones. I would think that evasion of one's true greatness is actually seen as a virtue in religious institutions. "Who am I to stand out?" Victor Frankl put it this way, "What is to give light must endure burning." In a sense, we fear this "burning" – this painful process of shifting from unchallenging, predictable life we're comfortable with to a demanding one that requires us to let go of the familiar, plunge into the unknown, and all too often "build our wings on the way down." The monotony of a caged, dull life may slowly kill us at the core, but the thought of jumping into the unknown gives us a very clear image of how we might suddenly die in the most painful way possible.

There is also the underlying fear of being seen by others as self-centered, arrogant, and living a life's that extraordinary and hence unacceptable. Here we reserve a special kind of ridicule and resentment against those who are more successful or talented than the majority. In presbyterates, we often punish our best talent and coddle mediocrity. There is a lot of pressure to conform, as mediocrity is granted more acceptance while giftedness often means being differentiated to the point of isolation, and standing out can mean getting shot down more easily because the target is clearer that way. It is understandable why many people would prefer succumbing to a simple life meeting their basic needs, and actually being rewarded by the institution for it, instead of battling it out in the bloody road towards self-actualization. Sometimes we set low aims for ourselves and call it virtue. The possibility of becoming remarkable shoots a thunderbolt of fear into many unremarkable people. Maybe our biggest sin is not what we do, but what we fail to do. Michelangelo put it this way. "The greater danger for most of us is not that our aim is too high and we miss it, but that it is too low and we reach it."

# CONCLUSION

*Being terrified but going ahead and doing what must be done – that's courage. The one who feels no fear is a fool, and the one who lets fear rule him is a coward.*

Piers Anthony

The purpose of this book was to share my experiences in such a way that they might inspire others to adopt the practice of "doing hard things for their own good" and experience in their own lives the marvelous opportunities that come from it. Rumi, a 13th-century Persian Sunni Muslim poet, jurist, Islamic scholar, theologian, and Sufi mystic, said it this way. "Don't be satisfied with stories, how things have gone with others. Unfold your own myth . . ." If the personal stories contained in this book do not inspire at least a few people to reflect on their own experiences when they have given into either courage or cowardice and the consequences of those choices, then I have failed.

The very writing of this book has been the latest time so far that I have stood before courage and cowardice, faced my fear and chose courage over cowardice. I suspect that I will have to overcome a similar tinge of dread when I see it in print, as I did with my first book. I realize that having my story "out there," might invite criticism, scrutiny or ridicule.

If you have not figured it out by now, I love quotes. For me they are the distilled wisdom of invisible mentors. I have especially been inspired by these words from President Theodore Roosevelt's 1910 speech at the Sorbonne in Paris.

"It is not the critic who counts; not the man who points out how the strong man stumbles, or where the doer of deeds could have done them better. The credit belongs to the man who is actually in the arena, whose face is marred by dust and sweat and blood; who strives valiantly; who errs, who comes short again and again, because there is no effort without error and shortcoming; but who does actually strive to do the deeds; who knows great enthusiasms, the great devotions; who spends himself in a worthy cause; who at the best knows in the end the triumph of high achievement, and who at the worst, if he fails, at least fails while daring greatly, so that his place shall never be with those cold and timid souls who neither know victory nor defeat."

I have always appreciated a similar insight from the Nobel Prize winning French surgeon, Alexis Carrel. "Man cannot remake himself without suffering for he is both the marble and the sculptor."

If I had let criticism stop me, I would not have done one-tenth of the things reported in this book. In fact, one of the threads running through the whole book is my willingness to stand up to the judgement of others and that criticizing voice in my own head that warns me to back off from challenges and go somewhere where I won't get hurt. Since it is irrational to expect everyone to approve of you, you just need to proceed with your life and accept the fact that little cuts and jabs are just part of the deal. The problem is often more about them than you anyway. In fact, I read somewhere that burlesque dancer, Dita Von Teese, once said, "You can be the ripest, juiciest preach in the world, and there's going to be someone who hates peaches."

On the other hand, I have received a tremendous amount of encouragement and support from people over the years, people who have found my experiences inspiring and even life-changing. I have been told by many people that, when I talk about my experiences, they feel I am "talking to them." – what is most personal is most universal?" I also understand that just telling people about "how bad I had it" without talking about "how I got over it" is not at all helpful.

Because of my deliberate choices to do the difficult thing and push myself to become my best self I have met so many people who impacted my life for the better. By God's grace I am able to use my gifts to touch people's lives and hopefully bring healing, affirmation and encouragement. After all, the choices I made were not merely for my advancement. They put me in places and situations where I could use my particular gifts and experience at the service of the Church and the people I served. It is never a one way street. I have received so much love and affirmation in return. For that I am so grateful.

In all my years I never set out to be "special." I just did not want to be "ordinary." I admire the words of Archbishop Ireland when he preached at the twenty-fifth jubilee of Cardinal Gibbons as bishop. "Let others tell of the many; I would tell of the few. I am tired of the common. The common! We are surfeited with it. The want in the world, the want in the Church, today as at other times, but today as never before, is for leaders who see farther than others, rise higher than others, act more boldly than others. They need not be numerous."

I have tried to live by the following principles of intentional growth. I honored and appreciated my upbringing but also dared to go beyond it. I disliked "half-assed" efforts in myself. I never gave up trying to make the most of what I was given. I understood that excellence is never an accident but always the result of intention, effort and thoughtful execution. I knew that there was no rescue party out looking for me and there was no one to blame, but myself, for how my life unfolded. To that end, I always tried to remember the words of Viktor Frankl. "The last of the human freedoms is the ability to choose one's response to any given situation." I know that life is about the freedom of responding to the challenge of creating myself – and with that freedom comes responsibility. I could not, and therefore did not, follow the path that most follow, but tried instead to go "where there was no path and left a trail."

This "whole life review" will hopefully inspire me going forward. I hope it will encourage me in challenging moments that are yet to come that I have been braver than I believed, stronger than I seemed and smarter than I thought. With what I have learned, I am going to try to make the rest of my life the best of my life. How can I keep from singing?

My life flows on in endless song;
Above earth's lamentation,
I hear the sweet, tho' far-off hymn
That hails a new creation;
Thro' all the tumult and the strife
I hear the music ringing;
It finds an echo in my soul —
How can I keep from singing?
What tho' my joys and comforts die?
The Lord my Saviour liveth;
What tho' the darkness gather round?
Songs in the night he giveth.
No storm can shake my inmost calm
While to that refuge clinging;
Since Christ is Lord of heaven and earth,
How can I keep from singing?
I lift my eyes; the cloud grows thin;
I see the blue above it;
And day by day this pathway smooths,
Since first I learned to love it,
The peace of Christ makes fresh my heart,
A fountain ever springing;
All things are mine since I am his —
How can I keep from singing?

Christian Hymn - Words by Pauline T.

# MEMORABLE QUOTES

It is not the critic who counts; not the man who points out how the strong man stumbles, or where the doer of deeds could have done them better. The credit belongs to the man who is actually in the arena, whose face is marred by dust and sweat and blood; who strives valiantly; who errs, who comes short again and again, because there is no effort without error and shortcoming; but who does actually strive to do the deeds; who knows great enthusiasms, the great devotions; who spends himself in a worthy cause; who at the best knows in the end the triumph of high achievement, and who at the worst, if he fails, at least fails while daring greatly, so that his place shall never be with those cold and timid souls who neither know victory nor defeat.

President Theodore Roosevelt

Ninety-nine percent of failures come from
people who have the habit of making excuses.
George Washington Carver

We have more ability than will power, and it is
often an excuse to ourselves that
we imagine that things are impossible.
Francois de la Rochefoucauld

There aren't nearly enough crutches in the world
for all the lame excuses.
Marcus Stroup

In normal life we hardly realize how much more we receive than we give, and life cannot be rich without such gratitude. It is so easy to overestimate the importance of our own achievements compared with what we owe to the help of others.

Dietrich Bonhoeffer

Cultivate the habit of being grateful for every good thing that comes to you, and to give thanks continuously. And because all things have contributed to your advancement, you should include all things in your gratitude.

Ralph Waldo Emerson

I have the immense joy of being man, a member of a race in which God Himself became incarnate. And if only everybody could realize this! There is no way of telling people that they are all walking around shining like the sun.

Thomas Merton

Tears have a wisdom of their own. They are the natural bleeding of an emotional wound, carrying the poison out of the system. Here lies the road to recovery.

F. Alexander Magoun

Every child is born blessed with a vivid imagination. But just as a muscle grows flabby with disuse, so the bright imagination of a child pales in later years if he ceases to exercise it.

Walt Disney

I want a life that sizzles and pops and makes me laugh out loud. And I don't want to get to the end, or to tomorrow, even, and realize that my life is a collection of meetings and pop cans and errands and receipts and dirty dishes. I want to eat cold tangerines and sing out loud in the car with the windows open and wear pink shoes and stay up all night laughing and paint my walls the exact color of the sky right now. I want to sleep hard on clean white sheets and throw parties and eat ripe tomatoes and read books so good they make me jump up and down, and I want my every day to make God belly laugh, glad that he gave life to someone who loves the gift.

Shauna Niequist

When you change the way you look at things, the things you look at change.
Wayne Dyer

Revenge is not always sweet, once it is consummated we feel inferior to our victim.
Emile M. Cioran

Before you embark on a journey of revenge, dig two graves.
Confucius

The best revenge is to be unlike him who performed the injury.
Marcus Aurelius

You can judge your age by the amount of pain you feel when you come into contact with a new idea.
Pearl Buck

Self-care is never a selfish act – it is simply good stewardship of the only gift I have, the gift I was put on this earth to offer others.

Parker Palmer

Too many people overvalue what they are not and undervalue what they are.

Malcolm Forbes

Self-absorption in all its forms kills empathy, let alone compassion. When we focus on ourselves, our world contracts as our problems and preoccupations loom large. But when we focus on others, our world expands. Our own problems drift to the periphery of the mind and so seem smaller, and we increase our capacity for connection – or compassionate action.

Daniel Goleman

Many churches of all persuasions are hiring research agencies to poll neighborhoods, asking what kind of church they prefer. Then the local churches design themselves to fit the desires of the people. True faith in God that demands selflessness is being replaced by trendy religion that serves the selfish.

Rev. Billy Graham

A Plan B life can be just as good or better than a Plan A life. You just have to let go of that first dream and realize that God has already written the first chapter of the new life that awaits you. All you have to do is start reading!

Shannon Alder

Most people who reach 65 or beyond look back on their lives in later years with regret. They wish they hadn't been as concerned about the little things and had spent more time doing the things they had wanted to do.

Ernie Zelinski

Make a radical change in your lifestyle and begin to boldly do things which you may previously never have thought of doing, or been too hesitant to attempt. So many people live within unhappy circumstances and yet will not take the initiative to change their situation because they are conditioned to a life of security, conformity, and conservation, all of which may appear to give one peace of mind, but in reality nothing is more damaging to the adventurous spirit within a man than a secure future. The very basic core of a man's living spirit is his passion for adventure. If you want to get more out of life, you must lose your inclination for monotonous security.

Jon Krakauer

We are perishing for lack of wonder, not for a lack of wonders. When I really stop to think about it, I am overcome with amazement at things as far ranging as heart surgeries, airplanes, internet communication, strawberries in winter, sewer systems, the way our lungs work, electricity, space travel, the ability to read and write and the fact that I live in a twenty-first century American city rather than a tenth century thatched-roofed hamlet. It all makes whining about almost anything seem so obscene!

G.K. Chesterton

We need quiet time to examine our lives openly and honestly – spending quiet time alone gives your mind an opportunity to renew itself and create order.

Susan L. Taylor

Not forgiving is like drinking rat poison and then waiting for the rat to die.

Anne Lamott

If you ask people what they've always wanted to do, most people haven't done it.
That breaks my heart.

Angelina Jolie

Tradition is about protecting the fire, not preserving the ashes.

St. John XXIII

The last of human freedoms is the ability to choose one's attitude in any given set of circumstances.

Viktor E. Frankl

How much more grievous are the consequences of anger than the causes of it.

Marcus Aurelius

Anger is an acid that can do more harm to the vessel in which it is stored than to anything on which it is poured.

Mark Twain

Men never do evil so completely and cheerfully as when they do it from religious conviction.

Blaise Paschal

Soon silence will have passed into legend. Man has turned his back on silence. Day after day he invents machines and devices that increase noise and distract humanity from the essence of life, contemplation, meditation... tooting, howling, screeching, booming, crashing, whistling, grinding, and trilling bolster his ego. His anxiety subsides. His inhuman void spreads monstrously like a gray vegetation.

Jean Arp

Silence is sometimes the best answer.

Dalai Lama

I've learned that people will forget what you said, people will forget what you did, but people will never forget how you made them feel.

Maya Angelou

Mediocrity is climbing molehills without sweating.

Icelandic Proverb

Great spirits have always encountered violent opposition from mediocre minds.

Albert Einstein

The moment one definitely commits oneself, then Providence moves too. A whole stream of events issues from the decision, raising in one's favor all manner of unforeseen incidents and meetings and material assistance, which no man could have dreamed would have come his way.

W.H. Murray

Even in the mud and scum of things,
something always, always sings."
Ralph Waldo Emerson

We find comfort among those who agree with us -
growth among those who don't.
American politician, Frank A. Clark

Beginning today, treat everyone you meet as if they
were going to be dead by midnight. Extend to them
all the care, kindness and understanding you can
muster, and do it with no thought of any reward.
Your life will never be the same again.
Og Mandion

For every complex problem there is an answer that
is clear, simple, and wrong.
H. L. Mencken

All that is necessary for the triumph of evil is
for enough good people to do nothing.
Edmund Burke

My life has been filled with terrible misfortune;
most of which never happened.
Michel de Montaigne

You are never too old to set another goal or
to dream a new dream.
C. S. Lewis

The unexamined life is not worth living
Socrates

The child must know that he is a miracle, that since the beginning of the world there hasn't been, and until the end of the world will not be, another child like him.

Pablo Casals

To all the other dreamers out there, don't ever stop or let the world's negativity disenchant you or your spirit. If you surround yourself with love and the right people, anything is possible.

American musician, Adam Green

It does no harm just once in a while to acknowledge that the whole country isn't in flames, that there are people in this country besides politicians, entertainers and criminals. There are a lot of people who are doing wonderful things, quietly, with no motive of greed, or hostility toward other people, or delusions of superiority.

American journalist, Charles Kuralt

Every now and then it helps us to take a step back and to see things from a distance. Nothing that we do is complete . . . . No statement says everything that can be said. No prayer completely expresses the faith. No Creed brings perfection. No pastoral visit solves every problem. No program fully accomplishes the mission of the Church. No goal or purpose ever reaches completion We are laborers, not master builders, servants, not the Messiah.

Blessed Oscar Arnulfo Romero

Life is an echo. What you send out, comes back. What you sow, you reap. What you give, you get. What you see in others, exists in you. Remember, life is an echo. It always gets back to you. So, give goodness.

Unknown

As a searching investigator of the integrity of your own conduct, submit your life to a daily examination. Consider carefully what progress you have made or what ground you have lost. Strive to know yourself. Place all your faults before your eyes. Come face to face with yourself.

St. Bernard

To make a difference in someone's life, you don't have to be brilliant, rich, beautiful or perfect. You just have to care.

Mandy Hale

There are things that we never want to let go of, people we never want to leave behind, but keep in mind that letting go isn't the end of the world, it's the beginning of a new life.

Unknown

When one door closes, another opens; but we often look so long and so regretfully upon the closed door that we do not see the one which has opened for us.

Alexander Graham Bell

We grow gray in spirit long before we grow gray in our hair.

Charles Lamb

Those who are lifting the world upward and onward are those who encourage more than criticize.

Elizabeth Harrison

Let us stop thinking so much about punishing, criticizing and improving others. Instead, let us rather raise ourselves that much higher. Let us color our own example with ever more vividness.

Friedrich Nietzsche

You need to be aware of what others are doing, applaud their efforts, acknowledge their successes and encourage them in their pursuits. When we all help one another, everybody wins.

Jim Stoval

Do not go gentle into that good night.

Dylan Thomas

Youth is a gift of nature, but age is a work of art.

Garson Kanin

A man is not old until regrets
take the place of dreams.

John Barrymore

Happiness is an inside job.

Dr. Bernie Siegel

Believe that you will succeed ... believe it firmly
and you will do what is necessary
to bring it to success.

Dale Carnegie

People with goals succeed because they know where they are going ... it's as simple as that.

Earl Nightingale

Men are not prisoners of fate,
but only prisoners of their own minds.

Franklin D. Roosevelt

The "Knots Prayer"
Dear God, please untie the knots that are in my mind, my heart and my life.

Remove the have nots, the can nots and the do nots that I have in my mind.

Erase the will nots, may nots, might nots that may find a home in my heart.

Release me from the could nots, would nots and should nots that obstruct my life.

And most of all, dear God, I ask that you remove from my mind, my heart and my life all of the "am nots" that I have allowed to hold me back, especially the thought that I am not good enough.

Amen!

Those who think they can and those
who think they can't are both right.

Henry Ford

A happy person is not a person in a certain set of circumstances, but rather a person with a certain set of attitudes.

Hugh Downs

What we see depends mainly on what we look for.

John Lubbock

If you keep saying things are going to be bad,
you have a good chance of becoming a prophet.
Isaac Bashevis Singer

You hear people complaining about this present day
and age because things were so much better in former times. I wonder what would happen if they
could be taken back to the days of their ancestors —
would we not still hear them complaining? You may
think past ages were good, but it is only because you
are not living in them.
St. Augustine

I cannot change the direction of the wind,
but I can adjust my sails.
Unknown

The greatest discovery of my generation is that
a human being can alter his life by
altering his attitudes.
William James

All things that resist change are changed by that
resistance in ways undesired and undesirable.
Garry Willis

The most fatal illusion is the settled point of view.
Brooks Atkinson

To get what you want,
stop doing what isn't working.
Dennis Weaver

The only constant in life is change.
Francois de la Rochefoucald

The interval between the decay of the old and the formation and establishment of the new constitutes a period of transaction which must always necessarily be one of uncertainty, confusion, error, and wild and fierce fanaticism.

John C. Calhoun - VP under John Quincy Adams


*On facing transitions in one's life . . .*
It's like being between trapezes. It's like Linus when his blanket is in the dryer. There's nothing to hang onto."

Marilyn Ferguson


My life changed once things changed in me.

Tyler Perry


Nothing gets better by leaving it alone.

Winston Churchill


God will not have his work
made manifest by cowards.

Ralph Waldo Emerson


Courage is being scared to death,
but saddling up anyway.

John Wayne


The giant in front of you is never bigger than
the God who lives in you.

Christine Caine


Everything you want is on the other side of fear.

Jack Canfield

Fear defeats more people than
any thing in the world.

Ralph Waldo Emerson

I am not afraid . . . I was born to do this.

Joan of Arc

I can do hard things.

Philippians 4:13

The cave you fear to enter
holds the treasure you seek.

Joseph Campbell

Do not be afraid. Do not be satisfied with mediocrity. Put out into the deep and let down your net for a catch.

Pope John Paul II

Christianity has not been tried and found wanting;
it has been found difficult and not tried.

G. K. Chesterton

Only those who risk going too far
can possibly find out how far they can go.

T.S. Eliot

Faint not nor fear, but go out to the storm and the action, trusting in God whose commandment you faithfully follow; freedom, exultant, will welcome your spirit with joy.

Dietrich Bonhoeffer
German Lutheran pastor, theologian, dissident anti-Nazi

The bravest thing you can do when you are not brave is to profess courage and act accordingly.

Cora Harris

May you not forget the infinite possibilities that are born of faith.

Mother Teresa

You have to decide what your highest priorities are and have the courage to say no to other things. And the way to do that is by having a bigger yes burning inside you.

Steven Covey

Preach the Gospel at all times.
Use words if necessary!

St. Francis of Assisi

It's time Christians were judged more by their likeness to Christ than their notions of Christ.

William Penn

It's a dangerous business, Frodo,
going out your door.

Bilbo - to Frodo in Fellowship of the Rings

It seems the necessary thing to do is not to fear mistakes, to plunge in, to do the best that one can, hoping to learn enough from blunders to correct them eventually.

Abraham Maslow

The greatest mistake we make is living in constant fear that we will make one.

John C. Maxwell

A fear of the unknown keeps a lot of people
from leaving bad situations.
Kathie Lee Gifford

A boo is louder than a cheer. If you have ten people
cheering and one person booing, all you hear is the
booing.
Lance Armstrong

Our deepest fear is not that we are inadequate. Our
deepest fear is that we are powerful beyond measure. It is our light, not our darkness, that most frightens us.
Marianne Williamson

When deep injury is done us,
we never recover until we forgive.
Alan Paton

Without forgiveness, there is no future.
Desmond Tutu

The weak can never forgive.
Forgiveness is the attribute of the strong.
Gandhi

People shouldn't worry about their status before
God at the moment of death. I don't think God
judges us at our weakest moments, but at our
strongest moment.
J. Moltmann

Forgiveness is a gift you give yourself.
Suzanne Somers

If you look closely enough, you will realize
that he is doing the best he can.
Kathryn Hepburn to her daughter played by Jane Fonda
in *On Golden Pond*, when she was terribly frustrated
with her aggravating, old father.

Taking offense is just as destructive
as giving offense.
Ken Keyes

To forgive is to set a prisoner free and
discover that the prisoner was you.
Lewis B. Smedes

Forgiveness does not change the past,
but it does enlarge the future.
Paul Boese

When you hold resentment toward another, you are
bound to that person by an emotional link that is
stronger than steel. Forgiveness is the only way to
dissolve that link and get free.
Catherine Ponder

Freedom is not the right to do what we want, but
what we ought. Let us have faith that right makes
might, and in that faith, let us, to the end, dare to do
our duty as we understand it.
Abraham Lincoln

So far as a person thinks, they are free.
Ralph Waldo Emerson

The more we express our gratitude to God for our blessings, the more he will bring to our minds other blessings. The more we are aware of to be grateful for, the happier we become.

Ezra Taft Benson

We can only be said to be alive in those moments when our hearts are conscious of our treasures.

Thornton Wilder

If you have nothing to be grateful for, check your pulse.

Unknown

Would you know who is the greatest saint in the world: it is not he who prays most or fasts most. It is not he who gives the most alms or is most eminent for temperance, chastity or justice; but it is he who is always thankful to God, who wills everything that God wills, who receives everything as an instance of God's goodness and has a heart always ready to praise God for it.

William Law

[The Jonah Complex is] . . . the evasion of one's own growth, the setting of low levels of aspiration, the fear of doing what one is capable of doing, voluntary self-crippling, pseudo-stupidity, mock humility."

Abraham Maslow - describing the Jonah Complex

So what if you make mistakes?

Pope Francis

With each passage of human growth, we must shed a protective structure (like a hardy crustacean). We are left exposed and vulnerable — but also yeasty and embryonic again, capable of stretching in ways we hadn't known before.

Gail Sheehy

One can have no smaller or greater mastery
than mastery of oneself.

Leonardo da Vinci

If I were to wish for anything... it would be for the passionate sense of what can be, for the eye which, ever young and ardent, sees the possible.

Soren Kierkegaard

Many people's tombstones should read,
"Died at 30. Buried at 60."

Nicholas Murray Butler

We should every night call ourselves to an account. What infirmity have I mastered today? What passions opposed? What temptation resisted? What virtue acquired? Our vices will abort themselves if they be brought every day to the shrift.

Seneca, Roman Philosopher

Start by doing what is necessary,
then what is possible,
and suddenly you are doing the impossible.

St. Francis of Assisi

A man does not have to be an angel to be a saint.

Albert Schweitzer

There is no clock, no matter how good it may be, that doesn't need resetting and rewinding twice a day, once in the morning and once in the evening. In addition, at least once a year it must be taken apart to remove the dirt clogging it, straighten out its bent parts, and repair those worn out. In like manner, every morning and evening a man who really takes care of his heart must rewind it for God's service.

St. Francis de Sales

Anyone who stops learning is old,
whether this happens at twenty or at eighty.

Henry Ford

When one has not had a good father,
one must create one.

Friedrich Nietzche

Holiness is not something that comes from doing good; we do good because we are holy. Holiness is not something we acquire by avoiding evil: we avoid evil because we are holy. Holiness is not something that follows from prayer: we pray because we are holy. Holiness is not the result of kindness: we are kind because we are holy. Holiness is not something that blossoms when we are courageous: we are courageous because we are holy. Holiness is not the result of character building: we build character because we are holy. Holiness is not a gift we obtain after a lifetime of service; we give service because we are holy.

Fr. John Catoir

Sanctity is not a matter of being less human, but more human than other men. This implies a greater capacity for concern, for suffering, for understanding, for sympathy, and also for humor, for joy, for appreciation of the good and beautiful things of life.
Thomas Merton - on "Sanctity"

Anyone can give up; it's the easiest thing in the world to do. But to hold it together when everyone else would understand if you fell apart — that's true strength.
Anonymous

It's often the last key on the ring
which opens the door.
Anonymous

Impossible things just take a little longer.
Philo T. Farnsworth

What you spend years building, someone could destroy overnight: build anyway! If you find serenity and happiness, they may be jealous: be happy anyway! The good you do today, people will often forget tomorrow: do good anyway! Give the world the best you have, and it may never be enough: give the world the best you've got anyway! You see, in the final analysis, it is between you and God – it was never between you and them anyway!
Mother Teresa

Adversity has the effect of eliciting talents which,
in prosperous circumstances,
would have lain dormant.
Horace

Nobody grows old merely by living a number of years. We grow old by deserting our ideals. Age may wrinkle the skin, but to give up enthusiasm wrinkles the soul.

Samuel Ullman

Do not look forward in fear; rather look forward with full hope. God, whose very own you are, will lead you safely through all things, and when you cannot stand it any longer, he will carry you in his arms. Do not fear what may happen tomorrow; the same good God who cares for you today will take care of you then and every day of your life. He will either shield you from suffering or will give you the unfailing strength to bear it. Be at peace, and put aside all your anxious thoughts and imaginations.

St. Francis de Sales

That which doesn't kill you, makes you stronger.

Friedrich Nietzsche

Moral indignation is jealousy with a halo.

H. G. Wells

A great deal of what passes for
current Christianity consists in denouncing
other people's vices and faults.

Henry H. James

One should examine oneself for a very long time
before thinking of condemning others.

Moliere

One can remain alive long past the usual date of disintegration if one is unafraid of change, insatiable in intellectual curiosity, interested in big things, and happy in a small way.

Edith Wharton

Be a force of nature instead of a feverish, selfish little clod of ailments and grievances, complaining that the world will not devote itself to making you happy.

George Bernard Shaw

For peace of mind,
resign as general manager of the universe.
Anonymous

I have studied many times the marble which was chiseled for me — a boat with a furled sail at rest in the harbor. In truth it pictures not my destination but my life. For love was offered me, and I shrank from its disillusionment; sorrow knocked at my door, but I was afraid; ambition called to me, but I dreaded the chances. Yet all the while I hungered for meaning in my life. And now I know I must lift the sail and catch the winds of destiny wherever they drive the boat. To put meaning in one's life may end in madness, but life without meaning is the torture of restlessness and vague desire — it is a boat longing for the sea and yet afraid.

Edgar Lee Masters in *George Gray*

The indispensable first step to getting the things you want out of life is this: Decide what you want.
Ben Stein

He not busy being born is busy dying.
Bob Dylan

This is the true joy in life, the being used for a purpose recognized by yourself as a mighty one; the being thoroughly worn out before you are thrown on the scrap heap.
George Bernard Shaw

Our culture has become most sophisticated in the avoidance of pain, not only our physical pain but our mental and emotional pain as well . . . We have become so used to this state of anesthesia that we panic when there is nothing or nobody to distract us.
Henri Nouwen

I have heard it said that heroism can be redefined for our age as the ability to tolerate paradox, to embrace seemingly opposing forces without rejecting one or the other just for the sheer relief of it, and to understand that life is the game played between two paradoxical goalposts: winning is good and so is losing; freedom is good and so is authority; having and giving; action and passivity; sex and celibacy; income and outgo; courage and fear. Both are true. They may sit on opposite sides of the table, but underneath it their legs are entwined.
Gregg Levoy in Callings

Most men lead lives of quiet desperation and go to their graves with the song still in them.
Henry David Thoreau

The saddest summary of life
contains three descriptions:
could have, might have and should have!

The change in emphasis in our relationships and our society from "me" to "we" will not erode individual rights, ability, achievement, freedom of expression or ownership in any way. Nor will it require that we relinquish our hard-earned cash or possessions, repudiate our economic system or overturn our democratic way of life. The only thing we will give up is the need to strive for individual achievement at another's expense.

Lynne Taggart

By running away from our loneliness and by trying to distract ourselves with people and special experiences, we are in danger of becoming unhappy people suffering from many unsatisfied cravings and tortured by desires and expectations that never can be fulfilled.

Henri Nouwen

We ask ourselves, who am I to be brilliant, gorgeous, talented and fabulous? You are a child of God. Your playing small doesn't serve the world. There is nothing enlightened about shrinking so that other people won't feel insecure around us. We were born to make manifest the glory of God that is within us.

Marianne Williamson

Opportunity is missed by most because it is
dressed in overalls and looks like work.

Thomas A. Edison

Death is not the greatest loss in life.
The greatest loss is what dies
within us while we live.

Norman Cousins

One must attend carefully to everything. If you
apply yourself carefully to what you do, great
springs of strength and truth are realized in you.

Thomas Merton

Besides the noble art of getting things done, there is
the nobler art of leaving things undone. The wisdom
of life consists in the elimination of nonessentials.

Lin Yutang

Correction does much,
but encouragement does more.

Johann Wolfgang Goethe

It's the Holy Spirit's job to convict,
God's job to judge and my job to love.

Billy Graham

I'd rather have sticks and stones and broken bones
than the words you say to me, cause I know bruises
heal and cuts will seal but your words beat the life
from me.

Dave Barnes in his song, *Sticks and Stones*

The biggest human temptation
is to settle for too little.
Thomas Merton


There is no need to go to India or anywhere else
to find peace. You will find that deep place of
silence right in your room, your garden or even
your bathtub.
Elizabeth Kubler-Ross


Believe those who are seeking the truth;
doubt those who find it.
Andre Gide


The truth will set you free,
but first it will make you miserable.
James A. Garfield


I believe that unarmed truth and unconditional love
will have the final word in reality. This is why right,
temporarily defeated, is stronger than evil tri-
umphant.
Martin Luther King, Jr.


Nothing in all the world is more dangerous
than sincere ignorance and conscious stupidity.
Martin Luther King, Jr.


The truth is "hate speech" only to those
who have something to hide.
Michael Rivero

It's discouraging to think how many people are
shocked by honesty and how few by deceit.
Noel Coward


From the cowardice that shrinks from new truth;
from laziness that is content with half-truths;
from the arrogance that thinks it knows all truth —
O God of Truth deliver us!
Unknown

I long to accomplish great and noble tasks, but it is
my chief duty to accomplish humble tasks as though
they were great and noble. The world is moved
along not only by the mighty shoves of its heroes,
but also by the aggregate of the tiny pushes of each
honest worker.
Helen Keller